D0437479

SOLOMON
ON SEX

SOLOMON
ON SEX

JOSEPH C. DILLOW

THOMAS NELSON PUBLISHERS
Nashville

Acknowledgement

The studies that resulted in this book were undertaken while I was with Christian Family Life. Through their seminars and counseling ministry, I was given the platform to develop and apply this material. Many thanks to the president of Christian Family Life, Don Meredith, Little Rock, Arkansas.

Fourth printing

Published in Nashville, Tennessee, by Thomas Nelson, Inc., Publishers and distributed in Canada by Lawson Falle, Ltd., Cambridge, Ontario.

Printed in the United States of America.

Scripture quotations are from the New American Standard Bible, © The Lockman Foundation 1960, 1962, 1963, 1968, 1971, 1972, 1973, 1975, and are used by permission.

Library of Congress Cataloging in Publication Data

Dillow, Joseph C
  Solomon on sex.

  1. Bible O.T. Song of Solomon—Commentaries. 2. Sex (Theology)—Biblical teaching. I. Title.
BS1485.3.D55   223'.9'06   77-1049
ISBN 0-8407-5117-6

CONTENTS

SOLOMON
ON SEX

CHAPTER ONE
SOLOMON'S SONG

Amid the current deluge of marriage manuals and sensational guides to liberated lovemaking, one small, beautiful book deserves all the attention the others are clamoring for, but it lies misunderstood and largely neglected. Few people realize the One who created us male and female also provided us with specific instructions as to how we best respond as men and women.

Who wrote the book?

The author is Solomon, King of Israel. The Song was apparently written during the early part of his reign when he was still a young man.

What are we reading?

Solomon's writing takes the form of a lyric idyll, a kind of love song. In a lyric idyll, speeches and events don't necessarily follow in chronological order. It's like a movie with several flashbacks; the story remains temporarily suspended while the audience views a scene from the past. This explains the lack of chronological sequence in the song.[1]

Another feature of lyric idylls is the chorus. This is an imaginary group that interrupts certain scenes to make brief speeches or to give warnings. The writer uses the chorus as a literary device to make transitions from one scene to another or to emphasize a point.

The book is a series of fifteen reflections of a married woman, Solomon's queen, as she looks back at the events leading to the marriage, the wedding night, and their early years together. These "reflections" are expressed in fifteen short love songs.

The story behind the Song

King Solomon lives in the tenth century B.C. He is Israel's richest king, and owns vineyards all over the nation—one of them close to Baalhamon in the northernmost part of Galilee, near the foothills of the Lebanon mountains. While visiting this vineyard, Solomon meets a country girl, Shulamith. She captures his heart. For some time he pursues her and makes periodic visits to see her at her country home.

Finally he asks her to marry him. Shulamith gives serious consideration to whether she really loves him and can be happy in the palace of a king, and finally accepts.

Solomon sends a wedding procession to escort his new bride-to-be to the palace in Jerusalem. The book opens as she is getting ready for the wedding banquet and the wedding night. The details of their first night together are erotically but tastefully described, and the first half of the book closes.

The second half of the book deals with the joys and problems of their married life. She refuses his sexual advances one night, and the king departs. She, realizing her foolishness, gets up and tries to find him, eventually does, and they have a joyous time embracing again.

While she lives at the palace, the new queen often longs for the mountains of Lebanon where she grew up. She finally asks Solomon to take her there on a vacation. He agrees, and the book closes with their return to her country home and their enjoyment of sexual love there.

The message and overview of the book can be summarized on the chart on page 197.

SOLOMON ON SEX

Symbolism of the Song

God could have used medical terms or slang in speaking of sex. But medical terms cause a sense of awkwardness, and we react negatively to slang. So God avoided both by expressing these delicate things in the language of poetry: symbols. Symbolism says more than medical or slang ever could, but without creating awkwardness or evoking negative reactions.

When it comes to explaining the meaning of the symbols, we will obviously have to use some medical synonyms. This problem faces any tasteful interpreter of the Song.

We will follow the oldest attested method of interpretation—the normal approach. We will take the Song at face value and see how it applies to us today.

Some writers seem hesitant to believe sex was intended by God for any purpose other than procreation. Therefore, they refuse to accept a normal interpretation of the book. God, they say, would never allow a book about sex (even in marriage) in the canon of Scripture. So the normal meaning of the Song was covered up ("It's a metaphor"), slid over ("Well, it doesn't *really* mean *that*") and allegorized ("It's a picture of God and his people"). The book *is* full of metaphors and other symbols, but was never intended to be an allegory. Instead, it is simply a picture of idealized married love as God intended it.

As an example of how absurd our interpretations can become when we reject the normal meaning of the symbols, some Jewish rabbis argued the book was an allegory of Jehovah's love for Israel. In this context the verse, "My beloved is to me a pouch of myrrh which lies all night between my breasts" (1:13) was interpreted to refer to the Shekinah Glory between the two cherubim that stood over the Ark in the Tabernacle. Some Christian scholars, following the same approach, concluded the Song spoke, instead, of Christ's love for His church. They held that the "pouch of myrrh . . . between my breasts" referred to Christ appearing between the Scriptures of the Old and New Testaments![2]

We want to remove these metaphorical mists and take a clear look at God's guidelines for sex, love and marriage. As we do, we want to also point to the source of answers for all other areas of problems in our lives: the Word of God. God has spoken authoritatively on sex through Solomon, and those who try His guidelines will find them workable and true.

9

Was Solomon qualified?

Solomon had three hundred wives and seven hundred concubines; how could he have anything to say about ideal monogamistic love? If Solomon really believed monogamy was the pattern God wanted men to follow, as he says in the Song, and if he really was so ecstatic about his relationship with Shulamith, his bride, why then did he continue in his lustful polygamy which led to his downfall? Some possible answers:

(1) If Solomon wrote this book while practicing polygamy, it would be a powerful argument against the fruitlessness and emptiness of having many wives. It would be a poem emphasizing the beauty of ideal love written by one who had experienced the opposite. He could write from experience that polygamy is not fulfilling as the way to find a maximum marriage.

(2) The fact that Solomon may have been a hypocrite doesn't necessarily disqualify him from writing about how he *should* behave. Solomon also wrote Ecclesiastes and Proverbs. Ecclesiastes, written with the warning that life apart from a relationship with God is like trying to catch the wind, demonstrates Solomon knew from experience the truth about God.

In Proverbs, Solomon also stresses that ideal marriage consists of one man with one woman. And he emphasizes again the abuses of riches. In actuality Solomon violated just about every precept he wrote about; is he therefore unqualified to write the book of Proverbs? If you teach your children about the wrongness of lying and anger, then catch yourself in a lie or a fit of anger, does that mean your teaching was not sound? In the same way, the fact that a polygamist wrote the Song of Solomon doesn't affect the value of the book as a guide to sexual love in monogamistic marriage.

(3) Because the Song describes Solomon when he was a young man, in the early years of his reign, it is possible the wives he had contracted at this time were taken in political marriages, and that he had not yet degenerated into lustful polygamy.

Other views

Insofar as the aim of this book is popular rather than technical, digressions into discussions of other viewpoints will not be undertaken. This in no way is intended as a slight to these serious alternatives[3] but is simply a concession to a more practical aim.

Hence, the framework outlined above will be assumed throughout the book and only defended at what seem to be particularly important points.

FOOTNOTES

1. Richard G. Moulton, "Lyric Idyl: Solomon's Song," *The Literary Study of the Bible* (London: Isbiter & Co., Limited, 1903), pp. 207-224.

2. H. H. Rowley, "The Interpretation of the Song of Songs," *The Servant of the Lord and Other Essays* (London: Lutterworth, 1952).

3. For a good discussion of other views of the Song consult the article by Rowley listed in the footnotes to this chapter or the article by David Hubbard in the *New Bible Dictionary*, ed. by J. D. Douglas (Eerdmans, 1962), p. 1204.

CHAPTER TWO
THE WEDDING DAY

(Reflections #1, 2, Song 1:1–14)

WHAT'S HAPPENING?

As Shulamith enters the splendid residence of the king, her feelings are mixed: she is awed by the beautifully bedecked ladies of the court, but is also joyously anticipating her first night with Solomon as the bride he has chosen from all the ladies in his realm.

WHAT DOES IT MEAN?

1:1 SPEAKER: The Song of Songs which is Solomon's

We are told this is the most beautiful and the best song of Solomon, who wrote 1,005 songs (I Kings 4:32).

1:2 SHULAMITH: May he kiss me with the kisses of his mouth

Shulamith is reflecting on how much she has desired Solomon's caresses and how she anticipates them on her wedding night.

1:2b SHULAMITH: For your love is better than wine

The Hebrew word translated "love" is *dodem*, which often refers to sexual love.[1] It speaks of caresses and kisses: Shulamith is sexually aroused and eagerly looks forward to feeling Solomon's body against hers.

In the Hebrew culture every joyful banquet of celebration is referred to as "wine." So when Shulamith mentions wine, she means Solomon's love gives her more joy and pleasure than all the celebrating.

1:3 SHULAMITH: Your oils have a pleasing fragrance

In Solomon's time, it was the custom to rub the body with oil after a bath in preparation for a festive occasion. Also, the Egyptians placed small cones of perfumed ointment on the foreheads of guests at their feasts; body heat would gradually melt the ointment, which then trickled down the face onto the clothing, producing a pleasant aroma. This practice was adopted by the Hebrews (Ps. 133:2).[2] Here Shulamith is reflecting on the erotic sensation of Solomon's perfumed oils.

1:3b SHULAMITH: Your name is like purified oil

Purified oil was highly prized. She is saying she prizes Solomon as highly, so that the very sound or thought of his name creates in her heart a longing for him. Also, his name flows smoothly over the tongue, just like flowing oil.

1:3c SHULAMITH: Therefore the maidens love you

She views Solomon as the most eligible bachelor in Jerusalem. Then too, a woman in love tends to imagine that everyone else loves her beloved because he is so outstanding!

1:4 SHULAMITH: The king has brought me into his chambers

She anticipates the delights of being with her love in his inner room.

1:4b CHORUS: We will rejoice and be glad; we will extol your love more
than wine. Rightly do they love you.

At this point the chorus bursts into open song, rejoicing with Shulamith. They agree with her that Solomon is worthy of great love. (Remember the chorus is imaginary; here it serves to bring out the bride's reflections on her wedding day.)

1:5 SHULAMITH: I am black but lovely, O daughters of Jerusalem

Now the chorus is personified as the daughters of Jerusalem (the court ladies and the concubines of Solomon). Shulamith, probably feeling them scrutinizing her unfavorably, compares her gypsy coloring acquired from an open-air life to that of the lighter complexions of the city maidens. Although she is different from the ladies in her outward appearance, she is confident that she is as beautiful as any of them.

1:5b SHULAMITH: Like the tents of Kedar

This refers to the tents made of valuable black goat hair that were used by the nomadic people of Kedar.[3] When bathed in the flood of the evening's golden light, these tents were strikingly beautiful.

1:5c SHULAMITH: Like the curtains of Solomon

Solomon's palace was hung with precious tapestries also made from the beautiful black goat hair. Shulamith intensifies the description of her beauty by comparing herself to these tapestries.

1:6 SHULAMITH: Do not stare at me because I am swarthy, for the sun
has burned me.

She explains to those who are staring at her that her dark complexion has been caused by exposure to the sun.

1:6b SHULAMITH: My mother's sons were angry with me; they made
me caretaker of the vineyards

14

The phrase "my mother's sons" would have been unusual if her father were still living; she would have called them "my father's sons" instead. So apparently her father died while she was still young, and her strict brothers made her work in the vineyards all day.

Though we are not sure where she grew up, a strong possibility is the mountains of Lebanon (Song 4:8). Solomon's vineyard at Baal-hamon was not far from the town of Shunem. Shulamith's name may have been taken from the name of this town, indicating the possibility that this was her home. Since her name could also be the feminine form of the proper name, "Solomon" (indicating she is the "other part of" the king), it is possible the poet wants the reader to see both ideas in the play on words.

1:6 SHULAMITH: But I have not taken care of my own vineyard.

As caretaker of a vineyard, she was a real nature girl: she was not able to primp and take special pains with her appearance ("my own vine- yard"). No Maybelline eyes or Jean Naté skin for her! But notice she was by no means unkempt, or Solomon would never have paid attention to her in the first place. The point is that her beauty was natural, not *1 Peter 3.3* contrived.

1:7 SHULAMITH: Tell me, O you whom my soul loves, Where do you pas- *Possibly* ture your flock, Where do you make it lie down at noon? *a flashback*

Shulamith mentally addresses her love, who is not present. She refers *Could have* to him as a shepherd for three possible reasons. *been her*

First, being a country girl, she is familiar with shepherds wending their *first words* way through the fields, carefully tending their flocks. *to Solomon*

Also, when Solomon first saw her on a visit to his vineyard at Baal- hamon he may not have worn his regal robes but dressed instead in a more casual style for his visit to the country; thus he could have re- sembled a shepherd.

And last, she thinks of him as the shepherd of Israel, tending to the affairs of his flock, the people of Israel. (Scripture often describes govern- ing as "tending sheep." The Messiah, of which Solomon is a type, is later represented in John 10 as the Good Shepherd. See also Ezek. 34:12-15.)

At this point in Shulamith's reflection, Solomon is absent, occupied with governing his people. In contemplating marriage Shulamith ponders the nature of her future husband's job (love him, love his work). Will she be able to locate him when she needs him after they are married? Will he be able to attend to her needs as well as the needs of the nation? She gives this serious consideration.

1:7b SHULAMITH: For why should I be like one who veils herself *involved of her feeling she has to search for him*

This refers to the practice of a harlot, passing through the streets heavily veiled, seeking an invitation.

1:7c SHULAMITH: Beside the flocks of your companions?

She gently warns Solomon that if she has to go out searching for him she will violate local propriety and might encourage overtures from other men including some of his companions. The very thought of appearing immodest or of encouraging the affections of other men is morally repulsive to her. She loves only one man, and does not want to even suggest she could have an interest in another.

1:8 CHORUS: If you do not know, *or "can not understand".* most beautiful among women, Go forth on the trail of the flock, And pasture your young goats by the tents of the shepherds.

The chorus advises her that if she is going to marry Solomon, she must realize he will often be about the affairs of state and thus be inaccessible to her at these times. If she can't accept this, she had better not marry him but return home to live the life of a country girl among the shepherds.

Applications for Today

The first section of the Song gives us a wealth of practical information we can use in the Twentieth Century. For example, we see that Shulamith, before her wedding, has pleasant thoughts of her future husband, anticipating sexual intercourse with him on the nuptial evening. She obviously was not afraid of sex nor did she have any preconceived notions that sex was dirty, sinful, or hurtful.

This sets a key note of the Song: sexual love between a man and his wife is proper and beautiful to the Father. Shulamith reflects on how aroused she was and how she had looked forward to making love with

#1 sexual love between h & w is good & beautiful.

Heb 13.4
"marriage bed is undefiled"

16

her husband on her wedding day. She had a "holy desire" for her husband.

On counting the cost

Shulamith was wise enough to comprehend a principle: before you say "I do," be sure to count the cost. In contemplating marriage to King Solomon, she probably had an imaginary conversation with herself which in modern vernacular went something like this:

"Wow! *Me* married to King Solomon! Wait til the other Shunem girls hear. 'Queen Shulamith' has a nice ring to it!"

"No, *you* wait a minute. This marriage you're about to jump into is not an all-expense-paid vacation in Jerusalem! Solomon is a *king*, not just one of the shepherds. He's the shepherd of all Israel."

"You mean he won't spend all his time gazing into my eyes and composing love poems about me?"

"You got it. He'll often be gone for hours, sometimes for days. And who will look after you? You think those palace pretties will take you under their wings?"

"I get it. I'll be the queen, and it'll be my job to take care of *them*."

"And everyone will be watching you, waiting to pounce on your mistakes. The lovely ladies will be quick to help you see where you might 'improve'."

"Here in the mountains I can find comfort walking through the forests, but I guess there won't be any cedars of Lebanon in the palace, will there? Maybe I could learn to like the sound of wind sighing through the marble columns . . ."

"Your simple country life will be *over*, girl! From the moment you finish the wedding banquet your life will take a new turn, and you can never go back. You can bet your bottom shekel it won't be easy."

"Yeah, maybe I'd make a better wife to Gezer the goat herder."

"But on the other hand, Solomon treats you like a queen. You know you're more than a political marriage to him. He's thoughtful, gentle, kind, considerate, strong, wise, tenderhearted—and he loves you."

"Gee, I almost forgot!"

"Solomon knows you'll miss the mountains, and that you won't be exactly at ease in the palace at first. But remember, he promised you trips to the country. And he even hinted he's planning a special place for you in the palace."

"Well, it's pretty obvious I have to make a choice: the life I'm used to or Solomon. I can't have both. Which one am I committed to?"

"Try asking which one you can't live without. Then commit yourself completely to your choice. Just be sure to check the loose ends before you tie the knot!"

"Thanks—I needed that."

Because she understands fully *before* marriage the life to which she is committing herself, Shulamith is able to make a decision of the will. She does not let her emotions blind her. So when the hard times come, she is prepared. She knows exactly what kind of life to expect because she has counted the cost.

Love always involves a sober evaluation of the cost of commitment to a relationship that may not always be easy. After all, it's "for better or worse." Ask yourself, "Can I learn to live with his or her lifestyle and vocation?"

If he's a salesman and you can't stand to be left alone, can you find ways to make use of this time? If you want your wife to be home, but she loves her job at the bank, can you come to an agreement as to what she should do? If he's a doctor, can you cheerfully fix him coffee and kiss him good-bye when he gets an emergency call at 3 a.m.? If he's a minister, will you learn to smile in your goldfish bowl and thank people for their advice as to your "proper" or "improper conduct?" If he wants to be a missionary to the jungle tribes of Brazil, can you leave your home, family and country to follow him where God leads?

Hudson Taylor, ninteenth-century missionary to China, realized his fiancée wasn't willing to go to China where God had called him. It was either follow his emotions, marry the girl, and not go to China, or follow God's leading and go to China without her. He chose the Lord. God honored his choice by giving him a rich harvest on the mission field and by blessing him with a wife who supported him and greatly helped his ministry.

Christ put it this way, "For which of you when he wants to build a tower, does not first sit down and calculate the cost, to see if he has enough to complete it? Otherwise, when he has laid a foundation, and is not able to finish, all who observe it begin to ridicule him, saying, 'This man began to build and was not able to finish!' " (Luke 14:28–30). The tower to which He was referring was very likely a vineyard tower. Shulamith, caretaker of a vineyard, knew how to count the cost—and she did.

But suppose you weigh all the factors concerning your future mate's

What if you don't realize this until after you've said, "I do?" Reject her is = reject God.

occupation, decide you can live with it and commit yourself to him or her. Then after you're married he or she changes his mind and decides to pursue another career. You didn't expect it. You're mentally not prepared. And you can't see how you'll ever be happy with the new job. What course do you follow?

Here is where love's tire hits the road. A wife in this situation can either nag and complain until her husband gives in, or go along with him in dutiful resignation ("Oh, Millie Martyr doesn't mind!"), or thank God for the situation and commit it to Him.

A husband can either announce to his wife what he is going to do, dictator-style, or capitulate to her because he can't stand to see her cry (or hear her nag), or commit the decision to the Lord and then, taking into consideration his wife's feelings, choose what he believes to be the best course.

Modest indeed

Shulamith, knowing her husband will be away a great deal, is concerned about what might happen should she have to search for him. Only "one who veiled herself," a harlot, went out looking for a man; respectable ladies stayed home and were sought after by men. Shulamith is afraid if she has to look for Solomon, her action might be misconstrued and will invite advances from other men. Not that they would mistake her for a harlot—everyone would recognize the queen, but they might realize she is alone and lonely and be quick to take advantage of the situation.

Shulamith wants to avoid *every appearance* of evil, and women today would do well to follow her example. In Shulamith's day the identifying mark of a lady of the night was her heavy veil. Today men can still recognize a lady who is hustling by the way she dresses. She may not go out actively looking for men, and she may not be able to admit even to herself she is trying to provoke a reaction by her manner of dress, but men still get the message. A neckline too low, a hemline too high, or an over-all line a half size too small are all noted by the male half of the population.

In a recent letter to a newspaper column a shoe salesman complained about what women wear—and don't wear—when they go shopping. He cited a young girl going braless, in a see-through blouse. And, he said, her father was with her.

Even though dressing suggestively is becoming increasingly common in our society, it is still suggestive. Men are still aroused most strongly

19

THE WEDDING DAY

Handwritten margin notes:

#3 don't show interest or even let it appear to be interest in other men / women.

er 3.3.
.2.9,10

#2 also: kind of like "If you aren't going to be satisfied w/ your husband, maybe you shouldn't get married." Some for men.

R REASONS women NOT BE MODEST?
1. wife needs reassurance & love
2. style conscious
3. bondage of lust
4. nieve

through visual intake, so women who provide a lot for them to take in should not be surprised if men make advances. If that's what you want, that's how you'll dress. If you don't, you won't.

Attaching special value to our "imperfections"

Most of us have something about us we don't like. Often these things are insignificant from the standpoint of eternal values, but their emotional impact can be devastating. Sometimes these "imperfections" are not really imperfections, but simply things which society considers to be "abnormal" or unacceptable.

In Shulamith's society, for example, it was apparently not in fashion with the court ladies to have a rough, dark complexion tanned by the summer sun. Her response to this potential source of social ostracism is instructive; she placed special value upon it. To her, it symbolized true wealth. She makes her imperfection analogous to something the society in which she lives values highly, expensive curtains and beautiful black leather tents, made of goatskin. Thus, that which is considered socially unacceptable, she asserts is really of great value. It all depends on one's point of view.

There is a sense in which real imperfections, viewed in divine perspective, can be a source of true wealth. Paul found this to be true of his "thorn." Some have suggested this was a disfiguring eye disease. But whatever it was, it caused him to learn dependence upon the Lord, and Paul rejoiced in it (2 Cor. 12:7–10).

Not long ago, I met a father whose son had a deformed hand and foot. Some of the toes were joined together at birth—a source of constant embarrassment to the boy. Naturally, his friends were careful to point out this particular "imperfection" whenever they got an opportunity.

This father had a valuable way of dealing with this problem. He helped the boy see this imperfection as something allowed by God for loving purposes to help fashion him into a Christ-like person (Rom. 8:28–29). Thus, this particular imperfection was part of a special plan by a loving God and hence became a symbol to the young man of God's special care and ownership. It symbolized the true wealth God desired to work into his life.

From a slightly different perspective, an adopted little Indian girl was called "princess" by her grandfather. In a day of unfortunate racial prejudice, this little girl is being brought up to regard her darker complexion as a sign she is a "princess"—one of special rank and position.

SOLOMON ON SEX

While working on the campus during the late sixties, I observed a new dress fashion among black students. Taught for years by white society that black is "imperfect," that kinky hair is ugly, black females (and males) developed an intense inferiority complex about their racial heritage. They finally countered this in the same way Shulamith did—by ascribing special value to the very things white society rejected. They began to dress like their queenly African ancestors and stopped straightening their hair. That kinky hair and black skin became symbols of their ancestry, of which they had every right to be proud.

Has it ever occurred to you that some of the things you feel the most uncomfortable about in your personality, heritage, body, or intelligence, are really indicators of special purposes God desires to work into your life? Can you view them as special signs of His love?

A wedding day in ancient Israel always included a wedding banquet. We have just entered into Shulamith's inner thoughts on the day of her marriage. The poet now directs our attention to her private conversation with her beloved as they recline at the banquet table.

AT THE BANQUET TABLE
(Reflection #2, Song 1:9–14)

> 1:9 SOLOMON: To me, my darling, you are like my mare among the char-
> iots of Pharoah.

Solomon assures his bride that to him she is as beautiful as his horses. To us this would hardly seem flattering, but it was music to Shulamith's ears! At that time in the Orient the horse was not a beast of burden, but the cherished companion of kings. Solomon loved horses and particularly Egyptian horses: he had 1,400 chariots and 12,000 horsemen (1 Kings 10:26). His mare must have been the most outstanding of all his horses, so he is telling Shulamith she is one in a million.

He calls her "my darling;" the Hebrew word is *vaghāh*. This word has the twofold idea of (1) "to guard, to care for" and (2) "to take delight in having sexual intercourse with."[3] By calling her this name, Solomon is indicating his desire to make love with her and is, at the same time, affirming his protective love and care for her.

> 1:10,11 SOLOMON: Your cheeks are lovely with ornaments, your neck
> with strings of beads. We will make for you orna-
> ments of gold with beads of silver.

Solomon says the jewelry she is wearing is lovely, but he will have made for her beads and ornaments even more valuable than these, made of gold and silver. Notice he is promising that little gifts and expressions of his love will continue *after* they are married.

1:12 SHULAMITH: While the king was at his table, my perfume gave forth
its fragrance. *even as they eat, his thoughts are on his beloved.*

The table here is a divan, a kind of round table where meals were eaten in a reclining fashion.[4] The perfume is nard, a very expensive fragrance with which Shulamith has anointed herself. She sees the fragrance wafting from her to the king as an expression of her love reaching out to him while they were reclining at dinner.

1:13 SHULAMITH: My beloved is to me a pouch of myrrh which lies all
night between my breasts.

This refers to an Oriental custom in which a woman would wear a small sack of myrrh, a kind of perfume, around her neck at night. All the next day a lovely fragrance would linger there. She is likening Solomon to that sachet of myrrh: whatever beauty and charm she has is brought out by him. His love brings out her beauty (the "fragrance") all day long.

1:14 SHULAMITH: My beloved is to me a cluster of henna blossoms in
the vineyard of En-gedi.

A cluster of yellow-white henna blossoms was often used as an ornament. She says that for her to have the privilege of calling Solomon her beloved is to her an ornament that makes her beautiful. En-gedi was the location of vine gardens Solomon planted on the hill terraces west of the Dead Sea. It was an oasis, in the midst of a desert. Solomon is similarly a refreshment to Shulamith.

To cherish and protect

#5 protection & love go hand in hand. Insight we can draw from this reflection deals with the relationship of love and protection. When Solomon calls Shulamith "my darling" he links his desire for her with his protective love and care.

Protection and love go hand in hand. A woman needs to feel protected because protection gives her security, and the more secure she is, the

SOLOMON ON SEX

freer she is to love unreservedly. Very often the woman who feels secure in her husband's love and protective concern takes great delight in sex with her husband.

Little things mean a lot

Solomon indicates he will be giving his beloved a little "love gift" of silver beads and golden ornaments. Little things mean a lot to most women, and they don't have to be gold or silver (though they can be!) Gifts add to the romance of a relationship. Whoever said romance has to die when the minister says "I now pronounce you . . ."?

Gifts might include anything from Arpege to a basket of fresh fruit. Men, how about some scented soap for her bath, bubble bath, or bath oil, scented candles for the bedroom, wild asters you picked on the way home, a mushy card (go on, she'll love it), two matched cups for the coffee you share, a negligee you'd like to see her in, or a poem you wrote for her. Use your imagination! The greatest gifts are those given for no other reason except to say, "I love you."

#6 Give little gifts to her.

One February 3 my wife came home to find an envelope full of money and a poem telling her I had saved the money so she could buy the clock she wanted. She was very appreciative—and particularly pleased there had been no "event" prompting the gift. Why, Valentines Day (which I forgot) was eleven days away!

An ancient emphasis

The ancients placed great emphasis on bringing all five senses to bear on their lovemaking. As Shulamith's reflection indicates, they had a particular emphasis on scent.

#7 Be more creative in your times of lovemaking bringing all 5 senses into play.

If you or I walked into Solomon and Shulamith's bedroom, it might have looked something like this: the wall would be lined with beautiful linen and satin curtains which were coated with scented powders to make the room smell erotic. The bedsheets were dusted with scented powders as was the clothing. Furthermore, their bodies were anointed with scented lotions. To top it all off, they probably burned incense, and thus the whole room was filled with smoke. (In fact, we would probably have choked!)

While these procedures may seem extreme to Western tastes, a watered-down version can be fun. Some night, men, send your wife to a specially-drawn tub of water while you put the kids to bed and do the

23

dishes. Just let her soak and relax all those tired muscles. Give her a copy of the Song of Solomon to read while she relaxes. Put some essence oils in the bath water and a scented candle in the bathroom. You might even try burning some mild incense to give the bedroom a romantic atmosphere. I think it's time we Christian brothers used some sanctified imagination around our homes.

Preparation for the wedding night

 # 8 Be carefully prepared for your first night.

In the next reflection, Solomon and Shulamith leave the banquet table and go to the bridal chamber for their first night together. A newly married couple entering into their first intercourse experience needs to be aware of certain things. Many a honeymoon has ended in total disaster simply because there was not an adequate understanding of sexual matters or because of unrealistic expectations and psychological fears.

I would suggest *Sexual Happiness in Marriage* by Herbert J. Miles, Ph.D. (Zondervan, 1967, cf. pp. 82-101). Dr. Miles is a sensitive and extremely practical Christian counselor who has an excellent discussion of sexual technique as related to the wedding night. Tim LaHaye in *The Act of Marriage* (Zondervan, 1976) has an excellent and detailed discussion of making love the first time. He gives numerous practical suggestions for the wedding night that would be quite helpful to any newly married couple (or even a couple that has been married several years!)

Fear of inhibition

#9 Men, be aware of the strong feelings of modesty in new brides.

A marriage ceremony doesn't automatically remove twenty-one years of emphasis on modesty from the minds of many new brides. Miles reports one out of five new brides found it extremely difficult to undress completely in front of their husbands on the wedding night—and refused to do so.

An excellent Christian counselor I know, a person who has had a very appreciated pre-marital counseling ministry, makes this suggestion to young couples for the wedding night: when they get to the motel, they are to draw a deep, relaxing bubble bath.[5] Let the new bride get into the bath first while the husband is in the other room. A candle lit in the bathroom, being the only light, will produce a warm, romantic atmosphere. As they relax together in the bathtub, they can discuss the day, talk, and even pray thanking the Lord for the gift of each other. As they communicate and share, the warm water drains away the tensions of the

24

day, and the bubbles sufficiently hide the wife's body so she is not immediately embarrassed.

They should then begin to gently stimulate each other under the water, hidden by the bubble bath! As the sexual tension and anticipation mounts, many of the initial inhibitions begin to melt away and a transfer to the bedroom is more natural. This particular counselor has had many young brides call him back several weeks after the wedding and say, "Praise the Lord for bubble bath! It was an excellent suggestion. Thank you."

While we have no way of knowing what kind of instruction Jewish mothers gave their daughters as preparation for their first night with their new husbands, it seems clear Shulamith has no serious inhibitions or negative attitudes. In the following reflections, we find a mature and sensitive young woman who is sure of herself and has a healthy and positive attitude toward sexual love.

FOOTNOTES

1. Franz Delitzsch, *The Song of Songs and Ecclesiastes* (Grand Rapids: Eerdmans, n.d.), p. 20.
2. *The New Bible Dictionary*, ed. J. D. Douglas (Grand Rapids: Eerdmans, 1962), p. 906.
3. Delitzsch, p. 32.
4. Robert Gordis, *The Song of Songs* (New York: The Jewish Theological Seminary of America, 1954), p. 43.
5. Don Meredith of Christian Family Life, Little Rock, Arkansas.

Wait to start hearing good reports from your wives.

CHAPTER THREE
IN THE BRIDAL CHAMBER

(Reflection #3, Song 1:15–2:7)

CONTEXT

The royal couple has left the wedding banquet and has retired to the bridal suite. In the ancient world, it was customary for a king to build a special bedroom for his new bride. As they enter the bridal chamber, Solomon begins his lovemaking to his wife with praise (1:15). She responds with greater praise (1:16–2:1). Solomon tops her praise of him (2:2) and she then outdoes his praise of her (2:3). Thus the lovers are mutually extolling one another's charms with increasingly powerful descriptions of one another's beauty.

It seems evident that this increasing level of praise is intended by the author to reflect the increasing level of their passion as their lovemaking progresses. This must be the intent because the end product of these praises is a request by Shulamith to be refreshed with raisin cakes and apples (erotic symbols) a reference to lovesickness (sexual passion), and a request to be embraced (fondled, 2:5–6).

Before going on to comment on the text itself, I think it would be appropriate to pause a moment and lay out some of the reasons for understanding these first three reflections as occurring on the wedding day and night.

Anticipation and fulfillment

There seems to be a theme of anticipation and fulfillment within the first three reflections. In 1:1–8 she longs to be in the bedroom with her husband and in 1:15–2:7 we find them in the bridal chamber. In 1:3, 4 she desires the king's caresses and in 2:6 she receives them. She anticipated sexual intercourse in 1:4 and experienced it in 2:4–6. This anticipation and longing for her lover is highly appropriate for the wedding day but would violate the entire ethic of the Song (as well as the rest of the Scriptures) if these reflections described pre-marital events. Thus, the longing and fulfillment motif seems to unite these first three reflections into a single unit describing the wedding day.

The banquet table

This reference to a banquet table (1:12) fits very naturally with a wedding banquet since this is a book about courtship, wedding, and marriage. It is therefore improbable that any common banquet would be meant.

The sexual intimacies described

There are many allusions to sexual intimacies that would be wholly inappropriate to a pre-marital scene. In 2:6 she requests that Solomon "embrace" her. Most Hebrew scholars agree this means to "stimulate sexually, or fondle."[1] Kramer notes an interesting parallel phrase in second millennium B.C. love poems. In the Sumuzi-Inanna love romance we find the phrase, "Your right hand you have placed on my vulva; Your left, stroked my head."[2] The parallelism seems too direct to be coincidental.

She also says she is "lovesick." This is a reference to high sexual passion.[3] Furthermore, raisin cakes and apples are frequently connected with sexual arousal. The great Hebrew scholar Jastrow comments, "The raisin is again because of its sweetness, an erotic symbol, like the apple in the following line to suggest that the lovesick maiden can be rescued from her languishing condition only by the caresses and embraces of her lover."[4]

In 1:2 she describes in anticipation (daydreaming) her husband's love skill. His love is "going to be" sweeter than wine. The word for love here is sometimes used to mean sexual love.[5]

The banquet hall

In 2:4 Shulamith comments that the king has brought her "to his banquet hall." The Hebrew literally translates, "house of wine."[6] Every banquet of pleasure and joy in the Hebrew idiom is, as we have noted, called by the name "wine."[7] The "house of wine" was a common oriental reference to the bridal chamber.[8] Thus, the text places us in the wedding night.

Her sexual awakening

In Song 8:5, which occurs years later, Solomon and Shulamith pass an apple tree as they walk along a country road. He comments that it was there that she was first "awakened"—introduced into the joys of married sexual love.[9] The awakening is associated in 8:4 and 2:6 with "fondling." In 2:6 Shulamith requests that ". . . his right hand embrace me," and then warns against the careless "awakening" of love in the following verse (2:7). Similarly, after requesting that "his right hand embrace" her in 8:3, she refers again to the careless "awakening" of love in 8:4. Then Solomon says it was under the apple tree where he awakened her (8:5).

This association with physical fondling suggests the "awakenings" in this book refer to that of sexual passion. Furthermore, this verb is used to mean a "violent awakening" whenever it is found in this form (Deut. 32:11). The word translated "awake" is used at least once in the Old Testament in awakening of sexual passion (Hos. 7:4). The only other place in the book there is reference to her being awakened under the apple tree is Song 2:3. If 8:5 explains Song 2:3 to be a sexual awakening, this probably places the first three reflections on the wedding night.

Having suggested this chronological order, let's take a look at the beauty of their first night together. First, a basic commentary provides

SOLOMON ON SEX

information on the meaning of the symbols and then some comments are made which are applicable to twentieth century marriage.

COMMENTARY

The scene that follows becomes more and more intimate as the bride and groom leave the wedding banquet and proceed to the bridal chamber. Although this is not explicitly stated, it is implied in 1:16 when she comments on the luxurious bed they are lying on. They have moved from the table (1:12) to the bed (1:18).

> 1:15 SOLOMON: How beautiful you are, my darling,
> How beautiful you are!
> Your eyes are like doves.

The dove is a symbol of innocence and purity; the appearance of the eyes an index of character. Hence Solomon says she is beautiful and pure—a virgin.

> 1:16 SHULAMITH: How handsome you are, my beloved,
> And so pleasant!
> Indeed our couch is luxuriant!

The fact that the Hebrew word for bed comes from a verb meaning "to cover" suggests that originally a bed was considered a covered or canopied couch. Certainly the canopied bed was common with Ancient Near Eastern Monarchs. Numerous illustrations in Egyptian wall paintings of this era depict a canopy over the bed of the Pharoah and his wife. At any rate, the richest man in the world would fashion a bed from the most luxurious material available, probably satin or silk.

> 1:17 SHULAMITH: The beams of our houses are cedars,
> Our rafters, cypresses.

As Shulamith lies on the luxurious couch, she observes Solomon's thoughtful preparation in constructing the bridal chamber. Because she comes from a rural background, Solomon has apparently outdone himself to construct a bedroom that would remind her of the open air and the country that she loved. Its cedar-beamed ceiling and cypress rafters create a separate world for them to enjoy away from the hustle and bustle of city life. Solomon constructed much of his palace with cedar beams from Lebanon (1 Kings 7:1–12). Furthermore, he built a separate house for his wife.[10]

Lebanon, Shulamith's home, is above all famous for its dense forest cover. These mighty cedars have become symbols of majesty and pride in biblical imagery. These cedars and conifers furnished the finest building timber in the ancient East and were sought by the rulers of Egypt, Mesopotamia, and Syria-Palestine. The most celebrated of such deliveries was that sent to Solomon by Hiram of Tyre for the temple in Jerusalem (1 Kings 5:6–9).

Solomon probably used some of this very timber to construct the bridal chamber.

> 2:1 SHULAMITH· I am the rose of Sharon,
> The lily of the valleys.

She likens herself to a tender flower that has grown up in the quietness of rural life. Sharon is a region between Tabor and the Sea of Galilee[11] in the neighborhood of Nazareth where Jesus grew up in northern Galilee (1 Chron. 5:16). The rose of Sharon was a flesh-colored meadow flower with a leafless stem which, when the grass was mown, appeared by the thousands in the warmer regions. Humbly describing herself as a meadow flower, she had understandable fears of being out of place, a common meadow flower in King Solomon's palace.

The lily of the valley is a beautiful red flower commonly found in Palestine.[12] She thinks humbly of herself in comparison to the king and alludes to herself as a common country girl.

> 2:2 SOLOMON: Like a lily among the thorns,
> So is my darling among the maidens.

Solomon takes up the comparison and gives it a notable turn. He says all the other maidens in Jerusalem are as thorns compared to her. As Shulamith entered the splendor of the palace she had apparently been struck by the beauty of the "maidens," the palace pretties. But Solomon says her nobility of character and virgin purity set her above all the sophisticated court ladies who have spent their lives "caring for their own vineyards."

> 2:3 SHULAMITH: Like an apple tree among the trees of the forest,
> So is my beloved among young men.

SOLOMON ON SEX

The tempo of their lovemaking has increased; they are now actively involved in their love play. Shulamith praises the erotic and sensual lovemaking ability of her husband. The apple tree is a very frequent symbol in the Near East for sexual love.[13]

In the Egyptian love song, "Song of the City of Memphis," a man says to his lover, "Her breasts are like mandrake apples."[14] Gordis, the Jewish commentator observes, "Raisin cakes, which were used in fertility rites (cf. Hos. 3:1), served like the apples as an erotic symbol on the subconscious level."[15] Zockler also sees the apple tree as a symbol of sexual passion: ". . . just as the sweet fruit of the apple tree serves to represent his agreeable caresses."[16]

The apple tree is used throughout the Song as a symbol for sexual love (cf. 8:5). In effect, then, Shulamith is telling Solomon what a skillful lover he is. He is an apple tree, skilled at making love.

2:3b SHULAMITH: In his shade I took great delight and sat down,
And his fruit was sweet to my taste.

As she sits (presumably on cushions in the bedroom) beneath Solomon's shadow—cast perhaps from a lamp in the room, she delightfully "tastes his fruit." Several different interpretations have been given for this phrase.

Some have said it refers to being refreshed by his presence as an apple refreshes a weary traveler.[17] However, in view of the obviously erotic nature of the symbols (raisin cakes, apples) and the context ("Let his left hand 'fondle' me), this seems unlikely.

Others have seen it as a reference to the sweet taste of his words and works which make a happy impression on the one who experiences them.[18] Others see the sweet fruit of the apple tree as a symbol of his caresses.[19] In other words, she "tastes" his sexual embrace.

In extra-biblical literature, "fruit" is sometimes equated with the male genitals[20] or with semen,[21] so it is possible that here we have a faint and delicate reference to an oral genital caress. At any rate, it seems to speak of the intense sexual enjoyment they share.

2:4 SHULAMITH: He has brought me into his banquet hall
And his banner over me is love.

As mentioned above, the "banquet hall" was a common oriental expression for the bridal chamber. The banner of a king was a long pole with a cloth attached like a flag. It spoke of the king's protective care.[22] As Shulamith sits in Solomon's shade (protective care), she immediately associates his "banner" with his love, since his love provides security, care and protection.

> 2:5 SHULAMITH: Sustain me with raisin cakes,
> Refresh me with apples,
> Because I am lovesick.

The phrase "I am lovesick" is literally "I am sick with love." She means that at this point in their lovemaking she is completely overcome with sexual desire. In order to alleviate the "lovesickness" she requests that Solomon sustain her with raisin cakes and apples (symbols of erotic love). In other words, she asks him to satisfy her sexually without delay!

> 2:6 SHULAMITH: Let his left hand be under my head,
> And his right hand embrace me.

Shulamith tells her husband exactly what she wants him to do in order to alleviate her lovesickness, or sexual passion. As they lie on the couch she requests that his left hand be placed under her head and his right hand embrace her. Delitzsch says the Hebrew word means "to fondle."[23] She desires him to fondle and stimulate her by touching her body. The description of the consummation of their love in sexual intercourse is reserved for a later section (4:16–5:1).

> 2:7 SHULAMITH: ~~I adjure~~ you, O daughters of Jerusalem,
> By the gazelles or by the hinds of the field.
> That you will not arouse or awaken ~~my~~ love
> Until ~~(she)~~ pleases.

a vow *"until it's appropriate."*

At this point the reflection abruptly ends with this warning addressed to the chorus, here personified as the daughters of Jerusalem. Remember they are a literary device, not a real group of people. Here they provide an "audience" to hear the warning. The words in parentheses are not in the original Hebrew and should be omitted. A proper translation would be: "That you will not arouse or awaken love until it pleases."

Gordis convincingly demonstrates that the oath taken "by the gazelles or by the hinds of the field" parallels the listing in some of the biblical books such as Esther and Ecclesiastes in which an attempt was made to

SOLOMON ON SEX

avoid the mention of the Divine name.[24] Hence, Shulamith replaces the customary oath "by the Lord of Hosts" or "by the Almighty" with a similar sounding phrase in Hebrew, "by the gazelles or the hinds of the field" choosing animals which symbolize love. It is likely that the Septuagint retained some recognition of Shulamith's oath by rendering the unique Hebrew phrase as "in (or by) the powers and the forces of the field."

The phrase "that you will not arouse or awaken love until it pleases" is difficult and has been interpreted in various ways. It has been suggested the statement is a warning against forcing love to develop prematurely; it should develop naturally.[25] However, there are no indications in the entire story of either her or Solomon attempting to "force" the relationship to develop. Delitzsch sees it as Shulamith's plea to the daughters of Jerusalem not to interrupt their embrace.[26] While this makes good sense in the context, it requires an unlikely translation of the verb "awake." Delitzsch would translate, "That ye arouse not and disturb not love Till she pleases." Robert Gordis suggests, "Do not disturb love while it is passionate, lit. 'while it desires'."[27] Again, the Hebrew word means "awaken" and not "disturb."

It seems more probable the passage is a warning against the awakening of sexual passion before "it pleases." Schonfield translates, "Do not wake, do not quicken passion, Before it is ready to stir."[28] This view is defended by Zockler.[29] He says Shulamith is giving a stray warning to the court ladies that they are not to plunge rashly and unbidden into the passion of love, that is to say, not before love awakens of itself ("til heart is joined to heart, til God Himself gives you an affection for the right man").

Although there are numerous other Scriptures that warn against pre-marital intercourse (1 Cor. 6:19), this passage seems slightly different. It is a warning against the arousal of sexual passion with anyone other than the person you feel God has definitely led you to marry. Sexual passion is not to be aroused until "it pleases"—until it is appropriate. While there is still some ambiguity about the phrase "it pleases" and one cannot be dogmatic about the meaning, this interpretation seems preferable for several reasons.

(1) The theme of pre-marital chastity is stressed in several other places in the Song, and its virtues are praised (Song 4:12,8:8–12). This interpretation of the warning thus fits well with a major theme.

(2) As demonstrated previously, the "awakenings" are most likely sexual awakenings. Furthermore, she was sexually awakened "under the apple tree" while in the "house of wine" (the bridal chamber) according

THE BRIDAL CHAMBER

to 8:5 and 2:3–6. Since in the context immediately preceeding the warning not to awaken love, Solomon and Shulamith are in the "house of wine" and she is being "embraced" it would seem that the natural connection would be the sexual awakening just described. Thus, the text becomes a warning against doing what Solomon and Shulamith have just done (made love), until "it pleases," (until a couple enters their own house of wine or bridal chamber).

(3) This interpretation explains two similar passages in the book. In all three cases the warning is not only connected with a physical embrace, but it comes at the conclusion of a sequence of reflections which leads naturally to a warning concerning a major theme of the book (pre-marital chastity). These passages, 3:5 and 8:4, will be discussed in the commentary to follow.

COMMENT

Bedroom atmosphere

As Shulamith gazes upon the cedar beamed ceiling in the new bridal chamber (1:17) she must feel touched by Solomon's creativity and thoughtfulness. Where does cedar grow in Palestine? In Lebanon! Solomon was trying to do something any married couple should consider: creating a bedroom with atmosphere.

Their bedroom created a "world-apart" atmosphere to which they could escape. Many wives decorate their bedrooms as if they were trying to impress the neighbors rather than create an atmosphere for their married love. On the other hand, some wives spend hours decorating the living room, kitchen, and the children's rooms. But "no one will see the bedroom," they say, so why spend all that time and money? Your husband will see it! Have you even considered creating an atmosphere conducive to romance for you and your husband?

In many homes, the bedroom becomes the household "garbage dump." When guests come for dinner, all the unfolded laundry, clothes baskets, and other debris is cast behind the bedroom door so the living room appears spotless. On a daily basis the average bedroom is often cluttered with perfume bottles, hair spray cans decorate the dresser tops, and if there is a desk, don't open it or the entire contents will spill out onto the floor. REAL ATMOSPHERE!

Many things could be done to enhance your bedroom's romantic

34

atmosphere. Some couples like fur bedspreads and a wood-beamed ceiling. A number of couples have testified to the new vitality introduced to their love life by a water bed. Others prefer a four-posted bed and softly quilted comforter; some desire a coordinated effect with matching drapes, wallpaper and bedspread. What you like is what is right for you! Together you should decide what you would like your love hide-a-way to look like and then get busy making it just that!

Solomon's and Shulamith's bed was no doubt covered with silk sheets. While that is financially out of range for the average couple unless they are a king and queen, satin sheets add a delightful feel to the bedroom atmosphere and are not prohibitive cost-wise. Reserve them for "special occasions" (like when your husband comes home from a lengthy trip).

There is no reason why bedroom lighting has to be plain old white light bulbs. If you have extra colored bulbs, such as red, amber, or blue, in the nightstand drawer, you can change the entire atmosphere of your love hide-a-way with a simple change of color. Candlelight is also a fun illumination in the bedroom. *Anyone* looks better by candlelight, and what better time to look your best? A scented candle adds an extra touch. Ferns and other plants provide a relaxing, warm atmosphere.

Music can be a real addition to your bedroom atmosphere. Why not channel the stereo into your love hide-a-way? One man I know recently surprised his wife by bringing her home after a date into a bedroom in which the stereo was playing some romantic music and the room was lit by scented candles. They began to dance to the music and share their love. As they danced they gradually disrobed one another and danced and talked in the nude for about thirty minutes before making love.

It is this kind of sensitivity and romance that brings the spiritual dimension of the intimacy of a relationship into the sexual experience. Too many husbands tend to divorce the physical aspect of their relationship from a total spiritual and psychological intimacy.

Privacy is very important to a romantic bedroom. If at all possible the master bedroom of your house should be very isolated from the rest of the house. A lock on the bedroom door is very important to most wives; total privacy is a key factor in reducing any inhibitions.

Both Solomon and his Shulamite bride need a retreat they can enjoy together to escape from the pressures around them. Solomon needs an escape from the pressures of state, and his bride needs the same in view of the pressures involved in being a queen. Your husband needs an escape from the pressures of work, and you need a retreat from your work or from the children.

35

She praised her husband's love skill

When in 2:3 Shulamith says, "Like an apple tree among the trees of the forest, so is my beloved among the young men," she is complimenting Solomon on his skill in making love. Would that many twentieth century wives were as wise!

Frequently in the marriage counseling room a wife will complain that her husband is routine, unimaginative, and unromantic in his lovemaking. A basic principle in getting him to improve is to emphasize what he does right—not what he does wrong! Skill in lovemaking is probably more intimately connected with a man's sense of masculine identity than a woman's skill is related to her feminine identity.

It is much easier for a woman to establish a sense of sexual identity than for a man. The basic biological functions of menstruation, breast development, changes in bodily form, nursing and bearing children, establish this at an early age. The man, on the other hand, has only one basic *biological* identity point as far as masculinity is concerned: his success in lovemaking. This is not to say this defines masculinity biblically—not at all! But it does explain a nearly universally observed difference between men and women. A man can only establish his identity by doing something. The woman, on the other hand, receives her identity passively as her native biological functions mark her so clearly.

Some have suggested this is a biological reason why males tend toward aggressive behavior and females lean toward more passive behavior.[30] There certainly seems to be some truth in this even though there is no biblical comment on it. If this is true, it helps explain why a man's sense of masculinity is so intensely tied to his success as a lover.

It is extremely important to most men that they feel successful in giving their wives sexual fulfillment. If he feels like a sexual failure, it can spill into many other areas of the marriage. This is why impotence or even premature ejaculation can be a crushing thing for a man. He takes a lack of response from his wife in a personal way that many wives fail to understand. When she doesn't express interest equal to his, he thinks she considers him a failure as a man. He has not succeeded in a male function that uniquely defines him as a male. Since a woman doesn't need sexual intercourse to define her as female, she might view her husband's reactions to her lack of interest as "childish."

If you want your husband to act like a man, make him feel like one! Continually compliment him on what a good lover he is. Anything he

36

does right, let him know! Furthermore, pray that the Lord will give you a ~pray for~ ~her!~ response pattern that perfectly complements your man. The extent to which you can make him feel like a success in his lovemaking affects his aggressiveness and self-confidence in the business world, his sense of masculinity, and his motivation to take over spiritual leadership in the home!

What are the limits?

My wife recently taught a seminar to about two hundred women on this subject of "How to be a Creative Counterpart." The last one and one-half hours of this two-day seminar deal with the biblical view of sex in marriage. ~#3 Work out your "limits" mutually.~

At the conclusion of the session, she passed out slips of paper and asked the women to write down any unanswered questions they didn't feel she had covered. One lady asked, "What are the limits God sets on sexual play between a husband and a wife? How far should I let my husband go?"

Her use of the word "let" is a sad comment on the vitality of their sexual life. (It kind of reminds you of high school, doesn't it?) It implies she is the keeper of the "sacredness" of sex while valiantly resisting the unsacred pressure of her husband. But her question often comes up. Three biblical principles would be helpful for each couple in setting their own "limits."

First, *unselfish love* must be the motive. This is clearly the thrust of 1 Cor. 13:4–7. Love turns to lust when a man or woman is obsessed by a particular form of sexual expression, when he or she can no longer be happy without it. I'm speaking here of forms of sexual expression other than sexual intercourse, such as the oral genital love mentioned above (2:3). Paul says, "Everything is permissible for me, but not everything is beneficial. Everything is permissible for me—but I will not be mastered by anything" (1 Cor. 6:12).

There is another aspect of the notion of unselfish love. Is your motive simply to use your mate for your own pleasure, or is your motive to bring him, or her, pleasure? Ask yourself that question the next time you want to insist on a particular form of sexual expression that does not appeal to your mate.

Secondly, it must be based on *mutual agreement*. Consider Phil. 2:1–4 in this regard:

THE BRIDAL CHAMBER

If you have any encouragement from being united with Christ, if any comfort from his love, if any fellowship with the Spirit, if any tenderness and compassion, then make my joy complete by being *like-minded*, having the same love, *being one in spirit and purpose*. Do nothing out of selfish ambition or vain conceit, but in humility consider others better than yourselves. . . . Each of you should look *not only to your own interests*, but also to the interests of others. Your attitude should be the same as that of Christ Jesus.

I once taught a Bible study on the Song of Solomon and after hearing my exposition of Song 2:3, one husband went home to his wife and said, "There! It's in the Bible so now you must do it!" He had totally missed the point.

The fact that some particular form of sexual expression is found in Scripture does not make it right for every couple. This will be stressed over and over again throughout the pages of this book. The issue is mutual agreement. The Bible is silent as to the question of limits. Each husband and wife are free before the Lord to work out pleasurable and meaningful forms of sexual play as long as they are within general biblical principles.

Many of the characteristics of Solomon's and Shulamith's relationship simply would not be in "character" for your relationship. Fine. God doesn't ask anyone to be something they are not. He does, however, ask us to work on our negative attitudes and try to be what our mate wants within the limits of our own personality. Thus, everything in this book will not apply to everyone.

The third biblical criterion for "limits" is quite simply, *mutual submission*. This seems an appropriate application of Eph. 5:21, ". . . and be subject to one another in the fear of Christ." While sexual relationships are certainly not in Paul's mind when he makes this statement, would not this verse apply here also? If it does, then a basis of limits would be your mate's desires.

If a wife prefers certain forms of sexual expression and her husband is hesitant or unwilling to meet her needs, he should work on his attitudes. Likewise, a wife who refuses to consider some particular form of sexual expression desired by the husband violates this principle of "mutual submission."

Obviously, our submission to Christ is not a "duty" but is in a spirit of joyful obedience. Once the great breadth of biblical "limits" are realized, it is proper to work on one's inner attitude to become all your mate desires. Obviously, immoral activities like wife-swapping are excluded from this principle of "mutual submission" by numerous other Scriptures.

They had a freedom of communication

A lady came in for counseling concerning some of the physical aspects of her marriage. Her concern was that in twenty years of marriage, she had never had an orgasm.

The counselor's first question was, "Have you and your husband ever really talked about this?"

"No," she replied.

"Well, have you ever explained to your husband exactly what you would like him to do to stimulate you?"

"No," she said, with quite a bit of emotion.

"Why not?" the counselor probed.

"Well, we just don't talk about it."

This dear lady had been experiencing twenty years of tension because "we just don't talk about it." She had been doubting herself as a woman and her husband doubted himself as a man because he wasn't able to bring his wife to an orgasm. Untold hurt, emotional pain, and frozen communication barriers had been experienced all because "we just don't talk about it." (In Appendix I, some helpful suggestions are given from a biblical and medical viewpoint toward overcoming orgasmic dysfunction, but communication based on mutual love and understanding is foundational.)

Notice the lovers in this chapter are very vocal in describing one another's charms (1:15,16), in describing the sexual pleasure the other is giving (2:3–5), and in describing what they want each other to do to stimulate them (2:6). Your partner may not know what you like unless you tell him or her. Don't keep your mate guessing, upset because he or she doesn't please you as you would like. Tell your mate exactly what pleases you, and let your mate take it from there!

#4 Communicate your likes & dislikes.

Do not awaken sexual passion until "it pleases"

Shulamith does an amazing thing from the point of view of today's attitudes about sex. She emphatically warns the daughters of Jerusalem not to become sexually involved with any man other than the one they intend to marry. This warning for maintaining chastity is repeated in 3:5

#5 do not "tease"?

not to be teased or tease

and 8:4; thus we know God wants us to pay special attention to it.

Why is the warning regarding pre-marital sex interjected here, in the midst of the love scene? Possibly because as she describes the beauty and freedom of love on the wedding night, she associates that freedom with pre-marital chastity. Thus a beautiful ethical setting for their wedded love is provided. Sexual love is only intended for one partner—the one God leads you to marry—and no one else.

As an orthodox Jewish girl she was raised in a home where pre-marital chastity was stressed (4:12, 8:8-12), yet she seems to have nothing but a healthy, positive attitude about sex in marriage. Sex education in the home is often an attitude communicated by the parents rather than actual information or rules regarding sexual behavior. Thus, a home with very specific standards will not produce children with negative attitudes about sex as long as the attitudes on sex and the spirit of the physical relationship between the parents is healthy. A child often picks up attitudes about sex from the spirit emitted by the parents.

It seems some evangelical Christians need to readjust their attitudes on sex along biblical lines. Not long ago an evangelical magazine had a cover photo of a young husband and his pregnant wife walking together down a beach. Believe it or not, many letters came to the editor expressing moral indignation and shock, threatening to cancel their subscriptions. The cover was considered "suggestive."[31]

When another magazine described a major denomination's report on sexuality, which included an affirmation that sex is fun, a woman wrote in to imply it was virtual blasphemy to call sex "fun" when God meant it to be "sacred."

Unfortunately some Christian wives tend to view sex as a duty, as something to be endured as part of being submissive to their husbands. They would never call sex evil because they believe the Bible and know God created sex. But, on the other hand, to call it "joy" is just too much. Therefore, they settle on the word "sacred," at the same time giving the impression it is something highly undesirable, a hush-hush subject one doesn't talk or think about.[32]

The Song of Solomon calls for some radical rethinking of the "Christian" view of sex in marriage. In this beautiful love story the twentieth century couple can find many points of contact with their marriage experience. Let's turn our attention in the next chapter to a Christian view of engagement as we glimpse Shulamith's reflections of their date life.

FOOTNOTES

1. Franz Delitzsch, *Commentary on the Song of Songs and Ecclesiastes* (Grand Rapids: Eerdmans, n.d.), p. 49.

2. Samuel Noah Kramer, *The Sacred Marriage Rite* (Bloomington: Indiana University Press, 1969), p. 105.

3. Robert Gordis, *The Song of Songs* (New York: The Jewish Theological Seminary of America, 1956), p. 51. See also, Dr. Otto Zockler, *The Song of Songs (Lange's Commentary*, 12 vols; Grand Rapids: Zondervan, 1960) Vol. V, p. 62.

4. Morris Jastrow. Jr., *The Song of Songs* (Philadelphia: J. B. Lippincott Co., 1921), p. 171.

5. Delitzsch, p. 20.

6. Hugh J. Schonfield, *The Song of Songs* (New York: Mentor Books, The New American Library of World Literature, 1955), p. 97. See Delitzsch, p. 42.

7. Rabbi Dr. S. M. Lehrman, *The Song of Songs (The Five Megilloth,* Hebrew Text, English Translation, ed. Dr. A. Cohen; The Sonzino Press, 1946), p. 1.

8. Jastrow, p. 170.

9. Jastrow, p. 229.

10. O. R. Sellers, "Palace," *The Interpreters Dictionary of the Bible*, ed. George Arthur Buttrick (4 vols.; New York: Abingdon Press, 1962), III, p. 620.

11. Delitzsch, p. 40.

12. Lehrman, p. 5.

13. R. B. Laurin, "The Song of Songs and its Modern Usage." *Christianity Today*, Vol., XI, No. 22, August 3, 1962, p. 10.

14. R. O. Faulkner, Edward F. Wente, Jr., and William Kelly Simpson, *The Literature of Ancient Egypt* (New York: Yale University Press, 1972), p. 99.

15. Gordis, p. 81.

16. Otto Zockler, *The Song of Songs (Lange's Commentary*, 12 vols., Grand Rapids: Zondervan, 1960), V, 62.

17. S. Craig Glickman, *A Song For Lovers* (Downers Grove: InterVarsity, 1977), p. 40.

18. Delitzsch, p. 42.

19. Zockler, p. 62.

20. Stewart Perowne, *Roman Mythology* (London and New York: Hamlyn Pub. Co., 1965), p. 78. See also Kramer, p. 105 for Sumerian parallels.

21. Kramer, p. 105 and 96.

22. *International Standard Bible Encyclopedia*, ed. James Orr (5 vols.; Grand Rapids: Eerdmans, 1939), I, 384.

23. Delitzsch, p. 45.

24. Gordis, pp. 27-28.

25. Glickman, p. 44.

26. Delitzsch, pp. 46-47.

27. Dr. Robert Gordis of the Jewish Theological Seminary of America, personal communication, Nov. 23, 1973.

28. Schonfield, p. 103.

29. Zockler, V, 63.

30. George F. Guilder, *Sexual Suicide* (New York: Quadrangle, The New York Times Book Co., 1973), pp. 14-25.

31. Cited by Letha Scanzoni and Nancy Hardesty, *All We're Meant to Be* (Waco: Word Books, 1974), p. 114.

32. Ibid., 114.

CHAPTER FOUR
A TIME OF PREPARATION

(Reflections # 4, 5, 6, Song 2:8–3:5)

CONTEXT

A review

The Song of Solomon, as we have seen, contains a series of reflections of a married woman, Shulamith, in which she remembers certain events leading to her marriage with Solomon as well as some problems they experienced in the early years of their marriage.

The first half of the book (1:1–5:1) consists of reflections on the wedding day. These reflections are stated in a series of poetic songs. In the first three we see Shulamith's reflections on the wedding day, the wedding banquet and her remembrances of the beauty of their first night together. This section closes with a warning against pre-marital sexual involvement (2:7).

The next three reflections close with the same warning (3:5). Thus, one of the controlling thoughts of both groups of reflections must relate somehow to the avoidance of sexual relations prior to marriage. In the first three reflections (1:1–2:7) the message seems to be that it is wise to abstain from pre-marital sexual involvement because to do so may jeopardize the beauty of sex in marriage.

The message of the second group of reflections (2:8–3:5) seems to be that it is wise to abstain from pre-marital sex because it tends to obscure one's objectivity in making the correct choice of a life partner.

The engagement period has three basic purposes according to these reflections.

First, it is a time of getting to know one another in ways *other* than sexual (2:8–14). Secondly, it is a time of coming to grips with the potential problem areas of a couple's relationship and establishing problem-solving procedures (2:15–17). Third, it is to be a time of seriously counting the cost of being married to this person (3:1–5).

Some important advice

Too frequently young people today get married on a wave of sexual passion, with no clear picture of the person they are committing their lives to. Consider the following vignette by Russell Dicks, a marriage counselor in Florida.

Assuming that sexual expression is irresistible, like a flood, many couples inevitably find themselves standing before a minister to be married. Minister: "Do you take this woman with all her immaturity, self-centeredness, nagging, tears, and tension to be your wife, forever?" The dumb ox, temporarily hypnotized by the prospect of being able to sleep with her every night, mumbles, "I do." Then the preacher asks the starry-eyed bride who is all of eighteen, "Do you take this man with all his lust, moods, indifference, immaturity, and lack of discipline to be your husband, forever?" She thinks that "forever" means all of next week, because she has never experienced one month of tediousness, responsibility, or denial of her wishes, so she chirps, "I do," in the thought that now she has become a woman. Then the patient minister parrots, "By the authority committed unto me as a minister of Christ, I pronounce you man and wife . . ." As he does, he prays a silent prayer for forgiveness, for he knows he lies. They are not now husband and wife and he knows that few of them ever will be. They are now legally

A TIME FOR PREPARATION

permitted to breed, fuss, bully, spend each other's money, and be held responsible for each other's bills. It is now legal for them to destroy each other, so long as they don't do it with a gun or a club. And the minister goes home wondering if there isn't a more honest way to earn a living.[1]

It is apparently to avoid this situation that this particular section of the Song of Solomon is written. Shulamith has been reflecting about the wedding day (1:1–5:1). As she daydreams about their first night together, her thoughts wander back to their dating relationship. She reflects on her thoughts as she awaits the wedding procession (Song 3:6–13).

In her daydreaming, she focuses on a walk in the country which seems to be the subject of the first two reflections of this section (2:8–14 and 2:15–17). She then recalls a dream she had during their engagement period (3:1–5) in which her concerns about being married to a king surface in her thinking.

COMMENTARY

A SPRINGTIME VISIT
(Reflection #4, Song 2:8–17)

It is possible that Shulamith is reflecting on her thoughts as she awaited the bridal procession of 3:6–11. She is recalling her memories of a springtime visit Solomon made to her mountain home in Lebanon.

> 2:8 SHULAMITH: Listen, my beloved!
> Behold, he is coming,
> Climbing on the mountains,
> Leaping on the hills!

These mountains are distinguished by a white limestone ridge and glittering snows that cap their peaks for six months of the year. For the Phoenician coastal cities the Lebanon mountain ridge formed a natural barrier to invaders from inland.[2]

The lower mountain slopes support garden cultivation such as olive groves, vineyards, fruit orchards and small cornfields. It was in a vineyard on one of the slopes in southern Lebanon and in northern Galilee that Shulamith worked.

As she sits in her country home on the slopes of these beautiful mountains she sees Solomon eagerly

> Climbing on the mountains,
> Leaping on the hills!

to visit her during their courtship.

> 2:9 SHULAMITH: My beloved is like a
>   Gazelle or a young stag.

These animals suggest speed and often sexual virility. Apparently Solomon is running to see his love.

> Behold, he is standing behind our wall,

Solomon stands outside the wall of the house and looks at her through the windows.

> He is looking through the windows,
> He is peering through the lattice.

The windows in poor homes were boards arranged like a lattice. They could be turned open and shut by turning the boards.[3]

> 2:10 SHULAMITH: My beloved responded and said to me,
>   SOLOMON: 'Arise, my darling, my beautiful one,
>   And come along.'

She now remembers Solomon's words in these prior meetings and recounts them here.

> 2:11 For behold, the winter is past,
>   The rain is over and gone.

It is springtime and Solomon is asking her to go for a walk.

> 2:12 SOLOMON: The flowers have already appeared in the land;
>   The time has arrived for pruning the vines,
>   And the voice of the turtledove
>   has been heard in our land.
> 2:13   The fig tree has ripened its figs,

45

And the vines in blossom have
  given forth their fragrance.
Arise, my darling, my beautiful one,
And come along!

2:14   O my dove, in the clefts of the rock,
In the secret place of the steep pathway,

Solomon describes her as a dove, a common symbol of gentleness and purity. The phrase "clefts of the rock" is a figurative reference to her home in the mountains. She apparently lived in a mountain defile. The wood pigeon builds its nest in the clefts of the rocks and other steep rock places. When Solomon designates the Shulamite as a dove in the clefts of the rocks, he is referring to the fact that she is far removed from the world around. This suggests her naiveté and rustic simplicity.

But note again, her remoteness from the world does not seem to affect her sexual relationship with her husband. She has not been exposed to any of the Hollywood images, the sexual temptation of the world, or the pressure to conform in the girls' dorm. She has not had the "benefits" of a liberal education to free her from her "primitive religious conceptions," or the "benefits" of living in a co-ed dorm so she could learn to "relate" to the opposite sex as "real persons." Even though she has missed all these tremendous "educational" opportunities, she has no problem relating to her husband.

Let me see your form,
Let me hear your voice;
And your voice is sweet,
And your form is lovely.

Solomon tells her why he wants her to join him in these springtime walks: he simply enjoys her presence. He loves to see her beauty and to hear her voice.

THE LITTLE FOXES
(Reflections #5, Song 2:15–17)

This reflection presumably occurs while they are on that springtime walk. As mentioned before, the lower slopes of the mountains where Shulamith grew up were covered with gardens and vineyards. As they

46

are walking on these slopes, they pass a vineyard and see some foxes ruining one of the vineyards by digging up the roots of the vines.

> 2:15 SHULAMITH: Catch the foxes for us,
> The little foxes that are ruining the vineyards,
> While our vineyards are in blossom.

The foxes burrowed and gnawed at the roots of the vines. Here the foxes seem to be a symbol of the little problems that gnaw at Solomon's and Shulamith's vineyard (their blossoming love for each other). Shulamith sees these foxes and uses them to ask Solomon to "catch" or help work at the little problems that threaten to hinder their love.

Delitzsch describes it this way: "This is a vinekeeper's ditty, in accord with the Shulamite's experiences as the keeper of a vineyard, which, in a figure, aims at her love relations. The vineyards, beautiful with fragrant blossoms, point to her covenant of love; and the little foxes, which might destroy these united vineyards, point out all the great and little enemies and adverse circumstances which threaten to gnaw and destroy love in the blossom, before it has reached the ripeness of full enjoyment."[4]

These little foxes are seldom more than fifteen inches tall and in digging their holes and passages they loosen the soil so the vines do not grow well. They are proverbial symbols of destroyers (Neh. 4:3; Ezek. 13:4).

How important it is that both big and little differences are resolved *before* marriage. If you cannot work out problems you *do* know about before you are married, it is almost certain you will not be able to resolve problems you do *not* know about until after you are married. This rural country girl has a lot of practical wisdom! Before marriage a husband and wife are often able to agree on the basics of life such as religion, education, and the meaning of the universe. After marriage, however, they discover they disagree on hundreds of subjects such as mealtime and toothpaste!

This business of keeping foxes out of vineyards is more difficult than it sounds. Vineyards in Palestine were surrounded by stone walls topped by a hedge. The families stayed in villages in the middle of the vineyards to protect them from wild animals. This demanded much perseverance; if the people failed to watch, the foxes would begin their work of destruction.

So then, Shulamith is not only encouraging Solomon to deal with problems they might already be experiencing but to take a firm stand against any further difficulties by nipping them in the bud.

A TIME FOR PREPARATION

In 2:15 she speaks of their love as a vineyard in blossom. She now continues her praise of their love in verse 16 and at the same time alludes to a problem she anticipates once they are married, Solomon's attendance to the affairs of state and the possibility of his neglect of her.

2:16 SHULAMITH: My beloved is mine, and I am his;
He pastures his flock among the lilies.

No shepherd would feed his sheep among lilies; that would be thieving! This must be another symbol referring to Solomon's attention to his flock, Israel. Shulamith, drawing on her background as a shepherd girl, uses the language of the country to give Solomon the highest praise she knows: he is a shepherd who feeds his flock among the lilies.

Lilies are an emblem of purity and beauty and of kingly stature. She is saying Solomon is a king who feeds his people, Israel, the best food available—righteousness, purity, and wisdom. He has the best interests of his people at heart. He leads Israel in the way of prosperity. The description of the king of Israel as a shepherd was so common in this agrarian society that Ezekiel even used it of the Messiah (Ezek. 34).

The verse brings together the basic tension she feels; the potential conflict between their commitment to each other (My beloved is mine, and I am his) and Solomon's commitment to the affairs of state (He pastures his flock among the lilies). This tension mushrooms into a major crisis later in their marriage (5:2-6:10). The next scene (3:1-5) indicates she had recurrent dreams about this problem.

This brings us to the question of what brought Solomon to her home for the springtime visit. It seems unlikely he would come all the way from Jerusalem just for a date. It seems more reasonable to assume the king was combining business with pleasure. While attending to some business of state in the mountains, he stops to spend a few hours with the woman he loves and hopes to marry someday. At the end of verse 16 their morning walk is about to end, and Solomon must attend to whatever business brought him north. The problem of separation is here illustrated again; she requests that he come see her again before he returns to Jerusalem after completing his business for the day.

2:17 SHULAMITH: Until the cool of the day when the shadows flee away,
Turn, my beloved, and be like a gazelle
Or a young stag on the mountains of Bether.

Return this evening when your work is through, says the Shulamite, and hurry back, (be like a gazelle, an animal noted for its speed).

Bether is not a proper name. It literally means mountains of division or separation. It probably refers to the intervening mountains Solomon must cross once again to get back to her that evening.

Before we leave this springtime visit, one final point of application is suggested. Solomon was the richest man in the world at this time. He could have spent hundreds of dollars on the Shulamite girl. But instead of spending money, he took her for nature walks in the Lebanon hills. When he appeared for their "date," there is no indication he brought her any elaborate gifts.

The important thing during courtship and engagement is not spending a lot of money in order to try to impress your partner or to purchase a good time. A dating relationship can be structured around inexpensive and creative fun (such as picnics by a river) that provide opportunities for each partner to really get to know one another and to talk out in detail their feelings about life, their commitment to Christ, and their basic views and backgrounds. The purpose of the engagement period should be related to getting to know your future mate well.

A DREAM—COUNTING THE COST
(Reflections #6, Song 3:1–5)

In the first scene she reflects on Solomon's arrival and the happiness she enjoyed when they were together. Perhaps as she reflected on Solomon's temporary departure until evening, her mind was drawn back to a recurrent dream which was so vivid that she remembers it as a real experience.

It is a dream of the painful longing that seized her when she lost the nearness of the presence of her beloved.

The dream occurred "night after night" (3:1) while she was in bed at her mountain home in Lebanon.

> 3:1 SHULAMITH: On my bed night after night I sought him
> Whom my soul loves;
> I sought him but did not find him.

She had a recurrent dream of what life would be like *after* she married Solomon. The dream reveals a nagging uncertainty as to whether she would be happy with a king whose time would be occupied with the affairs of state and who would often be away on business.

3:2 SHULAMITH: I must arise now and go about the city;
In the streets and in the squares
I must seek him whom my soul loves.
I sought him but did not find him.

In her dream, of course, she is living at the palace in Jerusalem. She goes into the streets to seek Solomon, but she cannot find him; so she asks the palace guards:

3:3 SHULAMITH: The watchmen who make the rounds in the city found me,
And I said, 'Have you seen him whom my soul loves?'

3:4 SHULAMITH: Scarcely had I left them
When I found him whom my soul loves;
I held on to him and would not let him go,
Until I had brought him to my mother's house,
And into the room of her who conceived me.

In the dream she pictures her home in the mountains and Jerusalem as close together. She finds her lover immediately upon leaving the guards and refuses to let him go until she has brought him to her home in the mountains. To this country maiden the most secure place she can think of is her mother's home where she was raised.

She wants to marry Solomon and live in Jerusalem, but she is not sure she can be happy away from her mother's home in the countryside. The dream seems to suggest that she would like to "have her cake and eat it too." In the city she feels she might be a country girl out of place. This could cause many feelings of insecurity and tend to cause her to be more possessive of Solomon's time than she knows she has a right to be. She has been seriously counting the cost of marrying Solomon.

The issue she is concerned with is, "Will I be happy married to a king?" The fact that the king desires her and that she would attain much prestige as a queen seems to play an insignificant part in her thinking.

The second group of reflections of the love song closes with a repetition of the warning against arousing sexual passion with any man other than the man God wants you to marry.

3:5 SHULAMITH: I adjure you, O daughters of Jerusalem,
By the gazelles or by the hinds of the field,
That you will not arouse or awaken my love,
Until it pleases.

(See discussion on 2:7.)

At this point in the Song she turns from her reflection on the dream and speaks to the imaginary group once again.

The first time the exhortation was given (2:7) was at the conclusion of a joyful and passionate love scene on their wedding night. By joining the love scene with the warning, the message seemed to be this: "If you desire to have the maximum sexual relationship in marriage, avoid any pre-marital arousal of sexual passion other than with the man God has led you to in engagement."

But what connection does the exhortation have to her reflection on their engagement days described here in the second group of reflections? The connection seems to be this. The arousal of sexual love with the *wrong* man can tend to hinder objective evaluation of whether or not he is the man that God has chosen for you.

Sexual passion has a way of sweeping a person into marriage or an emotional tie without getting to know each other first of all in ways other than sexual. The obsession of sexual desire tends to tempt a girl and guy to spend more time petting than working out the "little foxes" and problems that need to be worked through before the marriage commitment is made. Also, the power of aroused sexual passion can drive a couple to get married without giving serious thought to the problems of life with that person after you have said "I do."

Thus in view of the dangers involved and the seriousness of a marriage commitment, Shulamith warns not to arouse sexual passion until you have worked through the "little foxes," have thoroughly gotten to know one another in ways other than sexual, have counted the cost of marrying that particular person and have committed yourself to go through with the ceremony. Then and only then can sexual passion be aroused outside of marriage with the one whom God has brought into your life.

The message of these reflections can be summed up on the chart on the following page.

COMMENT

The relevance of this section of the Song to contemporary dating and engagement is obvious. There are, perhaps, four central points emphasized here that deserve expanded comment. These four points constitute four objectives of engagement as taught by the Song of Solomon.

GOD'S PURPOSES IN ENGAGEMENT		

Reflection #4
 	
to get to know
   each other
	Reflection #5
	
	to work through
	   problems
		Reflection #6
		
		to consider the
		   cost

"A springtime visit" 2:8 2:14	"Catch the little foxes" 2:15 2:17	"I sought him but did not find him" 3:1 3:4
3:5—In view of these factors, be sure not to arouse sexual passion until you are sure he/she is God's man or woman.		

To get to know one another in ways other than physical

As pointed out in the commentary, all these objectives of engagement are in some way related to the dangers of over-involvement in premarital sexual play. In the springtime visit (2:8–14) we find Solomon and Shulamith enjoying a walk in the vineyards without any sexual involvement (3:5). The Song expresses enjoyment of one another's company and delight to be in the presence of the beloved. It was, then, a time of simply getting to know each other.

One of the questions asked most frequently by young people is, "How do I know if he (or she) is the one?" The dating relationship is designed to help make that decision. There are a number of questions to which any young man or woman should give careful consideration before counting a particular person as God's choice.

First of all, there are questions about qualifications for marriage in general. Secondly, there are questions a young woman would want to have answer to in regard to a particular man she is considering marrying. Thirdly, there are some questions that a young man should ask that relate specifically to his potential bride-to-be.

Before reading this list of biblical characteristics of a future mate, a word of caution. After I showed this chapter to my wife, she commented, "If I had abided by this list, I never would have married you!"

Allow room for growth and maturity. There is no one who meets these standards, yet we should still use them to evaluate a future mate. Teddy Roosevelt once said, "It is not so important what a man is but what he is becoming, for he shall be what he is now becoming." When Jesus chose his men, he certainly had the standards of perfection in mind, but they were in many respects as far from the standard as one could imagine.

What they had was something of even more importance to Jesus—a devoted heart. The same is true in considering a list for evaluating a future mate. Is there a disposition of heart to be this kind of person?

Some general questions

First let's consider some general questions about any person's qualifications for marriage.

(1) Is he or she totally committed to Jesus Christ? The Bible prohibits marriage to a non-believer (2 Cor. 6:14ff.). It also discourages "missionary" dating. Dating a person in order to "win him for Christ" rarely works out. Generally people end up marrying someone they date. Therefore, if you date non-Christians you'll probably end up marrying one.

How can you tell if he or she is committed to Christ? Simply by observing his or her priorities. What consumes this person's life? Does he simply give lip service to being a Christian or does it consume his thoughts, time and actions? This quality is your only sure basis for a vital, growing, and trusting marriage relationship. Usually you can see where a person's heart is by looking at his closest friends. Are they excited about Christ? If they aren't, he or she probably isn't either. Of course, this doesn't mean a Christian won't have non-Christian friends, but usually his or her most intimate friends will be Christians.

(2) Does this person make you feel unconditionally accepted? If you feel you are on a performance basis now, it will get worse when you are married. The love described in 1 Cor. 13:4–7 is foundational to Christian marriage. It is an unconditional love.

One way you can tell whether this girl or guy will accept you unconditionally after you are married is to observe how he or she responds to the weaknesses of others right now. Right now you may experience unconditional acceptance; but if this person reacts negatively to the weaknesses of other people, then when you are married he will tend to react negatively to your weaknesses. If your weaknesses are met with negative responses, you will tend to clam up and not share your problems. As a result your desires for a sense of intimacy will be shattered.

With amazing regularity, men tend to treat their wives in a way similar to the way they treat their mothers, and women tend to respond to their husbands the way they did to their fathers. While there are many exceptions to this, it does suggest a careful look at the relationship this person has with his or her parents.

(3) Is this person able to respond with a blessing when hurt or offended by you or someone else?

> Do not repay evil with evil or insult with insult, but with a blessing, because to this you were called so that you may inherit a blessing (1 Pet. 3:9).

Peter's exhortation sums a section of his epistle in which he is dealing with marriage relationships. Many marriages get locked into an "insult for insult" type of reaction to each other. She hurts him; he hurts her back, etc. If you are dating someone who consistently renders insult for insult, be wary of marriage to that person.

(4) Is this person committed to God's priorities of family life? Briefly, a married person's priority list according to Scripture (see discussion to follow) is God first, mate second, children third, job and ministry responsibilities outside the home fourth. Consider what Moses said in regard to a new husband.

> When a man takes a new wife, he shall not go out with the army, nor be charged with any duty; he shall be free at home one year and shall give happiness to his wife whom he has taken (Deut. 24:5).

God is saying in no uncertain terms that a new husband's number one priority is his marriage—not a ministry for Christ or a vocation of a secular nature. That first year was so important that men were exempt from the draft. God saw it as more important for the country's welfare than fighting for her defense on the battlefield! That's because strong marriages make strong nations. That first year in particular is to be a building time for the rest of your lives together.

(5) Is this person financially responsible? Jesus taught that you can tell a lot about a person's inner spiritual life by how he or she handles money.

> So if you have not been trustworthy in handling worldly wealth, who will trust you with the true riches? (Luke 16:11)

In other words, there is a direct correlation between a person's receiving of "true riches" (spiritual vitality and insight) and his attitudes toward

SOLOMON ON SEX

money. When you find a man who is faithful in financial matters, you generally find that the rest of his life is in order. And conversely, when you find a man or woman who is undisciplined financially, this generally reflects on his or her whole life.

(6) Is this person committed to God's viewpoint on sex? Does this person demonstrate sexual control before marriage and does he or she have any views of sex that could cause you pain later on? This needs to be explored in a frank and open manner. Suggestions follow in the next section.

(7) Is this person submissive to constituted authority? Paul says husbands and wives should:

Submit to one another out of reverence for Christ (Eph. 5:21).

A person who does not have a submissive spirit will not fulfill this command in marriage. A man considering marriage to a Christian girl should ask whether she is willing to submit to him.

Wives submit to your husbands as to the Lord (Eph. 5:22).

If she will not "let any man tell her what to do," and seems generally bent on her career and so-called equality (which for the Women's Liberation Movement means equality of authority), and doesn't demonstrate a submissive spirit, think carefully about marrying her.

Even more important, if this man you are considering marrying does not demonstrate a submissive spirit toward constituted authority, you may be in for a life of pain if you marry him. As a Christian wife you are to submit to him in everything. If he is not submissive himself, you will resent this imposition and begin to fear yielding to him. You will become tired, due to nervous strain, your trust in him will decline, and you may even lose your sexual interest. It happens all the time. You can tell if he has a submissive spirit by observing his attitudes toward the school or university, government (Rom. 13:14; 1 Pet. 2:12ff), church (Heb. 13:17), parents (Eph. 6:1,2) and employer (1 Pet. 2:18–25; Col. 3:23,24).

Questions for young women

Assuming these general considerations that apply to any person have been considered, there are several specific questions a young woman

A TIME FOR PREPARATION

might ask from a scriptural viewpoint as she considers marriage to a particular man.

(1) Does he demonstrate that he has truly died to selfishness? (Eph. 5:25, Mark 8:34,35). One of the most important things a girl needs to do during a dating relationship is *listen*. Get that man to talk about anything and everything. As you listen, be sensitive to any evidence that he is selfish, living for himself, and prideful.

The Bible instructs husbands to love their wives as Christ loved the church and *gave Himself for her*. Christ was totally dead to his own desires and lived only for the will of the Father and for the good of his bride. If this man is incapable of unselfish love, do not let the relationship develop into a personal commitment. If he hasn't truly died to himself, you will find it extremely difficult to follow the biblical injunction to submit to him in everything. You will fear that your needs and the children's will not be met, and you will find it difficult to trust his decisions.

I have counseled too many women who married on a wave of sexual passion and are now regrettably locked into a paralyzing relationship with a man who is deliberately insensitive and selfish. The emotional pain these women endure is sufficient warning to any young woman not to be deceived on this point. You will not be able to hear the evidence of his selfishness if you are involved in a physical relationship with him. You can't "listen" very well "parking" in the back seat of a car!

(2) Does he set a spiritual example? (Mark 10:45; John 20:21; Deut. 6:4–10). If he doesn't do it now, it is highly unlikely that he'll begin to do it after you marry him. This will become extremely important to you when you have children and desire a genuine spiritual atmosphere in your home.

(3) Does he express a desire to protect you from dangers and difficulties? (Song 1:7; Rom. 7:2). In the Song, Shulamith refers to her husband as a "shepherd." The central emphasis of this imagery is leader and *protector*. When Paul speaks of a wife in Rom. 7:2, he uses a Greek word which means "a woman under a man." It carries the notion of being under her husband's authority and hence under his protection. A woman has a right to a "protective shield" provided by her husband. The male role is to be a kind of shock absorber. When things go wrong in the neighborhood, with the kids, with the finances, with the job, with the in-laws, etc., who absorbs the pressure? According to Scripture the husband is to absorb that pressure and remove it from his wife. When he doesn't (and too few men do), certain inevitable results follow. A wife

begins to develop tension headaches, she cannot respond sexually, and she is plagued by fatigue.

Does this man you are considering marrying lean on you for emotional support all the time, or do you have a freedom and confidence to lean on him? Are you always pumping him up emotionally, or is he a source of strength for you? If he's not your protector and shock absorber now, he won't be after you've said "I do." It will be extremely difficult for you to fulfill the responsibilities God has designated to you as a Christian wife unless he has this kind of ability.

(4) Is he able to provide for his future family? (1 Tim. 5:8; Gen. 2:24; 3:19). In order to maintain your respect and feel he is the leader in your home, he must have the confidence he can provide for his family's needs without depending on parents or others to do the job.

(5) Does he assume leadership responsibility in your relationship now? (Song 1:7; 1 Tim. 3:4,5). The notion of a shepherd also involves the notion of leader. God commands you to be a follower to your husband after marriage; can you imagine the frustration you'll be up against if you always have to prod and push? It may not bother you now; but after you're married it can be devastating. Many women begin to nag as a result.

(6) Does he demonstrate sympathetic understanding? (1 Pet. 3:7). Are you the one who always seems to have to be the understanding party? Does he communicate he really understands your deepest needs? If you don't have that feeling now, you'll be in for trouble after you're married.

(7) Does he give you honor? (1 Pet. 3:7). Is he proud of you? Do you get reports about how wonderful you are or about some accomplishments of yours? Many men do not make their wives feel queenly. They criticize and make cutting remarks in public.

(8) Does he cherish you? (Eph. 5:29). This is the word used of a mother tenderly caring for her baby (1 Thess. 2:7). The strong he-man types, loaded with "macho," are great fun to watch in the movies, but they often make lousy husbands. It is indispensable to a woman to know her husband is aware of her as a person, that she is cherished and valued and tenderly cared for. This involves small acts of chivalry; it involves noticing you when you walk into the room, and regular indications of thoughtfulness, such as gifts, flowers, etc. (Song 1:11).

(9) Does he demonstrate concerned involvement with your problems? (Matt. 11:28; Eph. 5:27). If you find his problems always seem to be the

A TIME FOR PREPARATION

topic of discussion, and his depressions or moods always seem to take precedence over your concerns, then you need to re-evaluate your commitment. After you are married and you have emotional problems, or conflicts with your boss, or difficulties with the children, and he never seems to be helpful, you'll understand what I mean. If he's not involved with you now, he may not be later.

(10) Is he at ease in demonstrating romantic love? (Song 4). I know a marriage right now that is on the verge of divorce simply because this man will not give his wife romantic love. He is emotionally paralyzed. Men are harmed by a lack of romantic love much less than women, and therefore cannot appreciate its importance to them. If a man is denied romantic love, he generally throws himself into his work and finds fulfillment there. Not so with a woman. A man may find an adequate life elsewhere, but a woman's whole existence shakes at the foundation. She suffers as no man can comprehend.

Many girls are shocked to find their boyfriends and fiancés were tender, romantic and affectionate prior to marriage, but within one month after the ceremony all the romance is gone. A girl needs to understand that for many men, much of the romance and affection they demonstrate prior to marriage is directly connected to the sexual reward they get by either holding you in their arms or petting. He may not be necessarily naturally that way at all. Consequently, when the sexual reward is no longer a "reward" but an ever-present item, he slips into taking you for granted.

So don't misread him on this point. Is he romantic when there is no sexual passion aroused in your relationship? Many wives complain, "I can always tell when he wants sex; he begins to get romantic. The only time he gives me any affection is when he wants to take me to bed."

These questions make the selection of a future life partner much more objective and rational. Obviously, intense physical involvement will seriously hamper your ability to think objectively about these crucial issues that can affect you and your children's happiness for the rest of your lives. Hence, God warns against pre-marital involvement.

Questions for young men

What are the questions that a young man should ask himself concerning a future wife? Solomon probably had a number of factors in mind during his springtime visits. He wanted to get to know her thoroughly before committing his life to her. He probably wanted to know at least these six things:

(1) Would she make a good mother to your children? If she doesn't ever want children or is offended by children, you could be in for some painful times. The average woman spends about 32 percent of her life (25 years out of 70) as a mother.

(2) Does she seem to respect you?

> However, each one of you also must love his wife as he loves himself, and the wife must *respect* her husband. (Eph. 5:33)

If she doesn't respect you, it could be your fault; you may not have the qualities that command a woman's respect. But if she is simply unable or unwilling to respect you, it will be difficult for you to derive a sense of self-confidence and self-esteem from her love. Likewise, it will be difficult for her to follow your lead.

(3) Is she willing to find her primary identity as your wife and the mother of your children and her secondary identity as a woman with a job or ministry outside the home? The husband's primary identity is outside the home and his secondary identity is in the home, according to the Bible. In other words, when she asks herself the question, "Who am I?" her first answer should be, "I am Bill's wife." This is what Paul meant when he said the woman was to be the glory of the man. To "be the glory of" is to derive one's significance from:

> A man ought not to cover his head, since he is the image and glory of God; but the woman is the glory of the man. (1 Cor. 11:7)

I realize that this runs counter to much modern thinking, but then modern thinking is resulting in a 50 percent divorce rate in the United States. Only when marriage is set up along God's principles of headship and submission will men and women be able to achieve their full potential as persons and be "all they were meant to be."

(4) Does she have a free and healthy attitude about sex like Solomon's wife Shulamith? Much marital pain occurs because wives take rather prudish and unscriptural attitudes about sex into marriage. They never work to overcome their inhibitions, requiring that a man perform like a super-sensitive romanticist, and demanding the "right to be left alone." Their lack of fun-loving response to their husbands' creative sexual imagination generates barriers, pain, and breaks up numerous marriages.

59

A TIME FOR PREPARATION

(5) Can she find joy in being a competent homemaker? (Prov. 31:11-31). Keeping house and being an expert at it can be a challenging and important job. Too many wives leave their homes in a shambles, dishes never done, and then lie around all day watching soap operas and wallowing in depressive fantasies.

Running an efficient home is a challenge and is some of the most important work of any member of the human race. That home sets an atmosphere in which children grow up—she creates "child soil." If you want that soil to be rich, be careful who you marry.

Housework can be done quickly after the children are in school, but many women turn it into a forty-hour a week drudgery and then complain about it.

Does this woman you are considering marrying look forward to creating a lively and warm home? If she thinks a career is more important, it could be a painful experience ten years from now.

(6) Is she industrious and a self-motivator? Consider in this connection the woman of Proverb 31.

> 31:13 She looks for wool and flax,
> And works with her hands in delight.

> 31:16 She considers a field and buys it;
> From her earnings she plants a vineyard.

She is a competent woman in business and real estate. She doesn't let the home "trap her," but she reaches outside the home into business interests.

> 31:20 She extends her hand to the poor;
> And she stretches out her hands to the needy.

> 31:24 She makes linen garments and sells them,
> And supplies belts to the tradesmen.

About 95 percent of the so-called "housewife syndrome" is self-imposed and has nothing to do with the traditional role relationship structure of the Bible as claimed by the Women's Lib Movement. All it takes is initiative and motivation to reach out. It may be with the poor, helping at a hospital, teaching Bible studies, speaking to women's groups, running child evangelism classes, helping with charities, or running a small business (or a large one!) If she's not industrious and

60

self-starting, she can become moody and depressed and tear down the entire atmosphere of a home. When a man comes home from the battle at the office all day, he wants a cheerful wife—not one who is moody and depressed.

This endless list of questions needs some qualification. There is probably not a man or woman alive who meets all of these standards. The issue isn't perfection, but where the heart's attitude is! It's not where you are, but the direction in which you are moving. Furthermore, it is probably just as important (if not more so) to focus on *being* the right person rather than *choosing* the right person. This list, then, also gives guidelines for being the right one.

To discern and resolve potential problems

The second objective of engagement suggested by the discussion of the little foxes (2:15-17) is that little problem areas must be resolved *before* the marriage. Frequently, these little problems can become major difficulties. May I suggest several little foxes that any engaged couple would do well to look at.

(1) Take a careful look at temperament differences. She may have a "leader," aggressive type temperament, and he may have a "follower" type temperament.

For a very valuable test to help open guided discussion in this area, seek out a pastor who can give you the Taylor Johnson Temperament Analysis test. (Published by Psychological Publications, Inc., 5300 Hollywood Boulevard, Los Angeles, California 90027). This test will visually map on graph paper nine basic temperament patterns and enable you to realistically see how you view yourselves and one another.

Also, it would be extremely beneficial to take the Stuart Marital Pre-Counseling Inventory. This is primarily geared for resolving marital problems, but it can be used to surface attitudes about various aspects of marriage and desired changes in one's future mate. This should be administered by a qualified pastor or Christian counselor. (Published by Research Press, 2612 N. Mattis Avenue, Champaign, IL 61820).

(2) Take a careful look at background differences. The man may come from a large, rollicking family with easy-going, untidy ways, and virtually no discipline. She, on the other hand, might come from a small family where there was stern discipline and little affection shown.

Now these two have decided to spend their lives together. They are going to share a bed, bathtub, and a tube of toothpaste. This small, neat girl who has always had her own small, neat bed and who always sleeps on her right side finds herself sharing a bed with a person twice her size who is used to fighting for the blankets with a younger brother. So he revolves like a windmill all night, winding the blankets tighter and tighter around himself. He continually leaves his clothes lying around the house and leaves the wet towel in a heap on the bathroom floor after taking a shower. He wakes up at six every morning raring to go. Her eyes don't even come into focus until ten, and he wants breakfast at six!

This is not just a nice visit; this is for keeps. They have to live together. Spend one of your "springtime visits" listing everything characteristic of your backgrounds, home environments, and economic statuses. Then spend the evening talking about each item on the list.

(3) Discern one another's aspirations and goals. An extremely profitable and enlightening evening can be spent discussing one another's dreams and goals. As an exercise, each of you write out a personal philosophy of life. Include your value system, your ambitions, what you consider the most important things in life, how you feel about entering into role relationship (submission for the wife, headship for the husband), what your fears about marriage are, and what you consider your strengths and weaknesses.

In view of the new emphasis on women's liberation, the question of role relationship takes on added importance. Is she willing to find her primary identity as wife and mother and her secondary identity in activities outside the home? Is she willing to acknowledge that her husband's career and job always takes precedence over hers?

(4) Discern one another's feelings about children and child discipline. How many children do you want? Many a young bride is shocked to find that her husband doesn't even want children.

Perhaps she came from a background where she was beaten continually, and the discipline was overbearing. He, on the other hand comes from a background where there was no discipline. Thus, when they formulate their philosophy of child discipline, he wants a lot of discipline, and she doesn't want any.

Numerous barriers develop over these issues. Talk about it before you get married. Read some good books on child discipline and discuss them. *Help I'm a Parent*, by Bruce Narramore (Zondervan, 1975) is a good one. Two of the best are *Hide or Seek*, by Dr. James Dobson (Revell, 1974) and *You and Your Child* by Charles Swindoll (Thomas Nelson, 1977).

(5) Discuss present relationships with parents and in-laws. All the jokes

62

about in-laws have some basis in fact. You are not just marrying a man; you are marrying into his family. Has he really left? Is he still dependent upon his family, and will he stand with you against them if need be? Is she likely to run back to Mommy every time there is a problem? Has she decided to totally break dependency on her family? If these decisions are not made, there can be a lifetime of trouble ahead.

Moses said, "For this cause a man shall *leave* his father and mother and cleave unto his wife and the two shall become one flesh." (Gen. 2:24).

(6) Are either of you financially in debt? Most judges will tell you the number two problem in marriages today, as evidenced by complaints filed in the divorce courts, is conflict over finances. If you are starting a marriage in debt, you are starting with some potentially problematic tensions.

(7) What are your attitudes about sex? Several dates could be spent discussing chapter by chapter *Sexual Happiness in Marriage* by Herbert Miles (Zondervan, 1967) or *The Act of Marriage* by Tim LaHaye (Zondervan, 1975). Frank, open discussion of the issues raised in these chapters is a must for beginning the marriage with open sexual communication. The number one cause of marriage breakup as far as complaints filed in the divorce court is sexual problems.

For a more technical exploration of this subject, I would suggest that you both take the Sex Knowledge Inventory published by Family Life Publications, Inc., Box 6725, College Station, Durham, North Carolina. This test surveys sex knowledge and sex attitudes and can be a very helpful tool in surfacing potential problem areas. Again, it must be administered by a pastor or marriage counselor.

To count the cost of marriage to this particular person

The third objective of engagement is suggested by the dream of separation (3:1-5). The dream reflects that Shulamith has been quite concerned about the possibility of being frequently separated from Solomon after they are married. This troubled her so much that she even dreamed about it. All this indicates she was seriously counting the cost of what it would be like to be married to a king. Before committing yourself for life, count the cost! There are at least three "cost factors" that everyone should objectively consider before entering into marriage.

(1) Since no one is perfect, you need to honestly evaluate your capacity to absorb the difference between where your potential mate is and where he or she ought to be, between the ideal of Scripture and the

reality of his or her present state of maturity. If you are unable to absorb that difference, don't marry that person. Sexual passion tends to obscure these issues. Many young people marry thinking, "I'll change him or her." The difficulty of actually living with that person is totally overlooked because of the sexual anticipation created through continuous petting and/or intercourse before marriage.

(2) Do you have the capacity to embrace his or her lifestyle and calling?

Here is a young couple, very much in love. She comes from an upper-class, socialite home. She was introduced as a debutante and has always moved in the circles of the very rich. She falls in love with a country boy who will never make the kind of money to support her in the style to which she has been accustomed. Nor will he ever move in the social circles she enjoys. Should she marry this man?

Or here is a young woman considering marriage to a medical doctor. She needs to count the cost of many lonely nights and midnight calls. Can she really be happy living that kind of life? If not, Shulamith warns, don't let a flood of sexual passion sweep these considerations under the carpet with the blindly naive notion that it will all work out somehow.

(3) Are you prepared to count the cost of re-arranging your personal time and priorities according to God's priorities in marriage and family life? God's priorities are as follows:

First, the development of a personal walk with the Lord

> But seek first His kingdom and His righteousness, and all these things will be given to you. (Matt. 6:33)

To put the Lord first does not mean putting your ministry before your wife and family. To put the Lord first means you put the development of personal fellowship with Him before your wife and family. It means you put your ministry and job *after* your wife and family.

Second, you must meet the needs of your mate.

> I would like you to be free from concern. An unmarried man is concerned about the Lord's affairs—how he can please the Lord. But a married man is concerned about the affairs of this world—how he can please his wife. (1 Cor. 7:32-33)

Your mate comes before your job or any business interests. Paul specifically commands husbands to:

> Love your wives, *just as* Christ loved the church and gave Himself up for her. (Eph. 5:25)

SOLOMON ON SEX

Besides His relationship to the Father, Christ's number one priority was the church. He gave Himself for her on the cross. Thus, a husband is likewise to place his wife as number one on his list of priorities (1 Tim. 3:5-8).

Third, you must meet the needs of your children. Your children come *after* your mate. Child-centered homes have destroyed numerous marriages and just about as many children. The best thing you can do for your children is to love your mate. Many sociological studies have confirmed it is more important to a child that Mommy and Daddy love each other than it is that Mommy and Daddy love the child.

Fourth, you must fulfill any job or ministry responsibilities outside the home. According to the Bible, the vitality of the home life is what gives a man the qualifications to have a ministry (1 Tim. 3:1-8). If your job is such that you cannot fulfill these other priorities to your wife's satisfaction, you should consider another job. God never asks a man to be a success on the corporate ladder, but he does ask him to be a success in his home. As far as working wives are concerned, the Bible is not against it as long as she meets the requirements of the other priorities to the mutual satisfaction of husband and wife.

If you don't think you would be able to commit yourself to these marriage priorities, that's fine, but you should realize that God may therefore be calling you to a single life.

FOOTNOTES

1. Reprinted by permission from HIS, student magazine of Inter-Varsity Christian Fellowship, © 1974.
2. *New Bible Dictionary*, ed. J.D. Douglas (Grand Rapids: Eerdmans, 1962), p. 726.
3. Franz Delitzsch, *The Song of Solomon* (Grand Rapids: Eerdmans, n.d.), p. 49.
4. *Ibid.*, p. 53, 54.

CHAPTER FIVE
THE WEDDING PROCESSION

(Reflection #7, Song 3:6-11)

CONTEXT

As if jolted by a sudden noise, Shulamith's daydreaming is abruptly focused on the gala wedding procession Solomon has sent to her home on the day of their marriage. Chronologically, this section comes before Song 1:1. After Shulamith sweetly remembers the joys of their first night together, she reminisces first of the days of their courtship and now of the glorious wedding procession. In Song 4, she once again turns her reflections to the wedding night.

Solomon has sent a bridal procession to bring his bride from the foothills of the Lebanon mountains in the north, to the palace in Jerusalem in the south. As the "scene" opens the wedding party is nearing Jerusalem; the speakers are evidently the chorus. They describe the wonders of the procession and thus make a transition from the dream of separation (3:1-5) to the events of the wedding night described in the next chapter.

COMMENTARY

3:6 CHORUS: What is this coming up from the wilderness
Like columns of smoke,

It is possible that the Chorus here is supposed to represent the inhabitants of Jerusalem who marvel at the gorgeous procession of their king marching toward the city.

Perfumed with myrrh and frankincense
With all the scented powders of the merchant?

As a wedding procession moved along, a censer of frankincense was swung at the front and back of the procession. Columns of smoke from the burning incense marked the beginning and end of the procession line.

3:7 CHORUS: Behold, it is the traveling couch of Solomon;

Presumably Solomon followed traditional Hebrew custom and picked up his bride at her home in Lebanon and then had her brought back to his palace in Jerusalem. Thus Shulamith is seated on the "traveling couch" and is being carried to the palace. This traveling couch was a box litter with poles projecting from the front and back and was carried on the shoulders of four to six men. It formed a bed upon which she reclined, and she was brought to Solomon in a cloud of incense.

3:8 CHORUS: Sixty mighty men around it
Of the mighty men of Israel.
All of them are wielders of the sword,
Expert in war;
Each man has his sword at his side,
Guarding against the terrors of the night.

Her way certainly led through the wilderness, and Solomon took special care to see she was protected against attack.

67

THE WEDDING PROCESSION

3:9 King Solomon has made for himself a sedan chair
   from the timbers of Lebanon.

As the bride approaches, the king is carried out to meet her on a "sedan chair" especially designed for the occasion. It is a couch long enough for the rider to recline, covered with a canopy and resting on pillars at four corners. It is hung around with curtains to exclude the sun and has a door, sometimes of lattice work, on each side.[1] As the bride approached Solomon's "sedan chair" she would enter it with him, and both would be carried to the palace.

3:10 He made its posts of silver,
   Its back of gold
   And its seat of purple fabric,
   With its interior lovingly fitted out
   By the daughters of Jerusalem.

The headboard to which the canopy was attached was gold, and the couch itself was royal purple, the color of kings.

The "daughters of Jerusalem" refer here to the court ladies who had lined the inside of the canopy with flowers intermingled with short sentences telling of the power of love.[2]

3:11 Go forth, O daughters of Zion,
   And gaze on King Solomon with the crown
   With which his mother crowned him
   On the day of his wedding,
   And on the day of his gladness of heart.

The women of Jerusalem collectively are addressed by the Chorus and called to behold their king. The crown here is not a symbol of royalty but of happiness. In ancient times garlands were worn on festive occasions, especially marriages.[3] His mother wreathed a fresh garland around the head of her youthful son. "The men have already welcomed the procession from afar; but the king in his wedding attire has special attractions for the women—they are here called upon to observe the moment when the happy pair welcome one another," Delitzsch comments.[4]

COMMENT

This beautiful little song suggests several points of practical application to marriage today.

SOLOMON ON SEX

Marriage involves public attestation

This is simply taken for granted here in that it follows traditional Hebrew custom. In the varied morality of our society, the question frequently comes up: "What constitutes marriage biblically?"

I'll never forget an evening that my wife and I spent with a charming young college couple who had been living together for over a year. They had just received Christ. They were not "married." What were they to do? Did God want them to stop counting each other as man and wife even though they had been living together as such for over a year? It was obvious by the way they related to each other that they were truly committed for life and were deeply in love. Should they separate now and call their relationship fornication?

Or consider a couple who have been "living together" for four years. During two of those years they were legally married to someone else. They are now divorced but very much in love. They then become Christians, open the Bible, and it says that they are not to get a divorce. Are they still married to their former mates? Should they go back?

These are difficult questions. They are made difficult because we have strayed so far from God's norms. In the case of the second couple, if they are legally married to the person they are living with now, they are prohibited from returning to their former mates (Deut. 24:1-4). What constitutes marriage as far as the Bible is concerned? Unfortunately, the Bible doesn't state it as specifically as we like. It more or less assumes certain things.

(1) *A commitment to leave the parents*. "For this cause a man shall *leave* his mother and father, and *cleave* to his wife; and they shall *become one flesh*." (Gen. 2:24). Thus, leave, cleave, and one flesh mark three prerequisites of marriage. To leave involves a break of dependency upon the parents and other in-laws. Too many marriages today are harmed because one mate continually sides with his or her parents against the other mate. Or a wife continually goes back to her parents and undermines her husband's authority and trust. This commitment means that, if necessary, the person must be willing to stand with his mate against his parents.

(2) *A commitment to cleave*. The Hebrew word translated "cleave" has the notion of "to stick like glue." It implies a permanent and unbreakable relationship. Thus, a basic prerequisite of marriage is a commitment to one mate for life. Casual promiscuity prior to marriage does not make one married to that person.

THE WEDDING PROCESSION

(3) *Sexual intercourse.* Becoming one *flesh* involves a sexual union. This is what consummates the marriage. Sexual intercourse apart from the above mentioned commitments does not constitute marriage.

(4) *A public attestation.* Throughout the Bible there is an emphasis on obedience to the constituted rulers and authorities. If the rulers require a legal license, the believer is bound to meet that requirement. Malachi 2:14 speaks of God's hatred of divorce. The prophet describes it as dealing treacherously with the wife of one's covenant, or mutual public promise. References on obedience to ordained authorities are many (1 Pet. 2:13-25; Rom. 13:1-7). In Song 3:6-11 we find Solomon and Shulamith attesting their marriage *publicly* (the only way it's ever done in the Bible).

However, the second factor—to cleave—seems to be the most important and perhaps the only indispensable prerequisite.

These four points describe a general biblical picture of marriage for which there may be legitimate exceptions. For example, a public attestation may not always be possible. A couple could be legally married and yet violate the first condition of *leave.* But ideally, these four factors seem to constitute the prerequisites of marriage from the biblical viewpoint.

Public attestation is important

We are all familiar with the type of bridegroom who stalwartly maintains he will endure the public ceremony because everyone knows the wedding day is for the bride. It's simply an unnecessary inconvenience he must go along with.

Solomon's elaborate preparations for the procession display an interest in the wedding itself. This interest can come across as saying, "Honey, you're a beautiful bride, and I want everyone to know how lucky I am."

A modern groom, on the other hand, who demonstrates no interest in the wedding or its preparation indicates the attitude, "I want to marry you, but . . . this is such an awkward situation, and I don't like weddings and . . . I wonder if it's worth it." The bride can pick up the unfortunate attitude that he is unwilling to sacrifice for her, even that he is not proud of her.

A wedding is a time of being set apart, a time for the bride to be shown off and admired by all. If the groom makes it seem an ordeal, it's as though the effort of showing off his bride is too great for him to bear. Grooms-to-be, take an active interest in the wedding plans. Even ask if there is anything you can do to lighten the load your bride will be carrying. If she desires it and it is possible, go with her to pick out the flowers, cake, etc., as well as china and silver. Make fun outings out of these ventures.

FOOTNOTES

1. Rabbi Dr. S. M. Lehrman, *The Song of Songs, The Five Megilloth*, ed. Dr. A. Cohen (The Soncino Press, 1946), p. 12.
2. *Ibid.,* p. 12.
3. *Ibid.*, p. 12.
4. Franz Delitzsch, *Commentary on the Song of Songs and Ecclesiastes* (Grand Rapids: Eerdmans, n.d.), p. 70.

CHAPTER SIX
THE WEDDING NIGHT

(Reflection #8, Song 4:1-5:1)

CONTEXT

In Chapter 1:1-2:7, we find Shulamith's memory lingering tenderly on their first night together and the events of the wedding day. Then, in the window of her mind, she begins to reflect on the events leading to the marriage. Her thoughts of the wedding procession naturally lead her to thoughts of their first night together. In this chapter we have an extended description of their lovemaking on the wedding night.

It is difficult to be certain this is the wedding night, but the close proximity with the wedding procession in the preceeding chapter tends to imply the wedding night is intended. It is possible, however, that this chapter describes another lovemaking experience months later in their marriage.

Thus, we assume the wedding ceremony occurred between chapters three and four. Also, the events of chapter one with Shulamith in the palace and later at the banquet table all occur chronologically before this song but after the arrival of the wedding procession.

The royal couple is alone. Solomon outdoes himself in praising the beauty of his bride. The beautiful love song in this scene gives us a glimpse into the consummation of their marriage.

The time of the scene seems to be late afternoon or early evening (4:6). (We must remember that for the ancients, the day ended much earlier than it does for us.) It appears that the wedding procession arrived sometime in the morning or about midday. Shulamith was then taken to the palace where she prepared for the wedding banquet. There we met her in the opening verses of the book. In mid-afternoon the wedding banquet was held. Now the afternoon draws to a close and twilight comes. The bride and groom retire to the bridal chamber eagerly antici-pating the consummation of their love in intercourse.

COMMENTARY

> 4:1 SOLOMON: How beautiful you are, my darling,
> How beautiful you are!
> Your eyes are like doves behind your veil;

Presumably Solomon and his bride, on the couch in the bridal chamber, have initiated their loveplay. Solomon is overwhelmed by the beauty of his bride and begins to praise her charms as his eyes and caresses pass over her body.

A dove (with which he symbolizes her eyes) is a traditional symbol of purity, innocence, and beauty.

The reference to the veil most likely does not refer to the veil that covers most of the face. Even though Delitzsch[1] seems to think it does, several factors make this improbable.

(1) It seems rather unnecessary and even awkward for a bride to remain veiled on her wedding night. The veil was to seal her off from the eyes of other men, not from her husband.

(2) The text clearly states that Solomon could see her teeth (4:2), her lips (4:3), her cheeks (4:3), and her neck (4:4), all of which would be covered by the oriental veil. Jews used a piece of silk or other material to cover women's faces.

In view of this, it seems preferable to take the suggestion of Lehrman[2] and others that the veil here refers to her hair cascading down her head.

Thus, the long hair of his Shulamite bride hangs across her face like a veil, but between the strands of hair he sees and praises her beautiful features.

Now prepare yourself for some seemingly unflattering praise.

4:1 SOLOMON: Your hair is like a flock of goats
That have descended from Mount Gilead.

If a modern husband said that to his wife on her wedding night, he'd either be met with tears or a purse hurled in his direction.

This is a metaphor of subjective response. Many times poets use certain metaphors in order to create a subjective response in the mind and emotions of the reader. In this particular case, these goats refer to black goats with long silky hair that glistens in the twilight sun. As they wound their way homeward coming down the restful slopes of Mt. Gilead, they created a sense of restfulness and beauty in the eye of the beholder. Solomon is saying Shulamith is like that. As he beholds her hair and her general beauty, he is overwhelmed with a sense of quiet. He loves to just look at her and take in what he sees. He's actually being quite romantic.

4:2 SOLOMON: Your teeth are like a flock of newly shorn ewes
Which have come from their washing;

To liken her teeth to sheep is to say they are as white as snow. To say that they are like newly shorn ewes suggests they are smooth. The allusion to the "washing" suggests that her teeth glisten with saliva.

All of which bear twins
And not one among them has lost her young.

All her teeth are twins; they come in pairs, top and bottom, and are evenly matched. Not only that, but she still has all her teeth—she has lost none of "her young."

4:3 SOLOMON: Your lips are like a scarlet thread,
And your mouth is lovely.

Shulamith apparently used lipstick of some type and other cosmetics in a comely way which highlighted her natural beauty.

SOLOMON ON SEX

It is very difficult to imagine that Solomon's words are separate from the parts of her body he is carressing. It would seem rather awkward to simply stare at her without caressing the parts of her body he is describing.

Thus, he starts his lovemaking by kissing her hair, teeth, and lips and stroking these areas as well.

Next he kisses and caresses her temples or cheeks.

Your temples are like a slice of pomegranate
Behind your veil.

Her rosy cheeks veiled by her hair resemble the pomegranate when cut open.[3]

The preceeding verse likened her charms to the rustic background from which she came. But she is not only a country maiden; she is the wife of the king of Israel. Hence, the following features are likened to things associated with Solomon.

4:4 SOLOMON: Your neck is like a tower of David
Built with rows of stones,
On which are hung a thousand shields,
All the round shields of the mighty men.

To liken her neck to a tower of David speaks of her erect and queenly carriage. The shields refer to the ornaments that normally adorned her neck as she walked in public. Shields were often hung on the outside of a tower wall to protect the tower. He is saying she is a source of strength to him. He needs her strength and encouragement.

4:5 SOLOMON: Your two breasts are like two fawns,
Twins of a gazelle
Which feed among the lilies.

Delitzsch comments, "The breasts are compared to a twin pair of young gazelles in respect of their equality and youthful freshness, and the bosom on which they raise themselves is compared to a meadow covered with lilies, on which the twin pair of young gazelles feed."[4]

The imagery suggests her breasts are uncovered.

It is interesting to observe how otherwise brilliant Hebrew commentators will allow their cultural preconditioning to rejct the obvious meaning of some of the passages of the Song. Zockler, for example, the brilliant German exegete says concerning this verse:

A more detailed parcelling out of the comparison, as for instance . . . by Weissb, who supposes a particular reference in the young gazelles to the dark colored nipples of her breasts as their especial charm, and in the lilies to the snowy whiteness of her bosom is inadmissible, and leads to what is in violation of good taste or to what is obscene.[5]

Delitzsch and others believe the text teaches what Zockler asserts to be in violation of good taste. Zockler rejects this interpretation because to him it appears obscene. This is not an exegete speaking. It is a man conditioned by his culture so that probable interpretations of the Song are ruled out by cultural preconditioning and not by hermeneutical principle. Others might see nothing in violation of good taste or obscene, but on the contrary, something beautiful.

The symbolism of gazelle and lilies is actually quite delicate and very beautiful. The reference was to the dorcus gazelle,[6] an animal about two feet high at the shoulders, and a marvel of lightness and grace. The beauty of its eyes was proverbial. One of the most common associations with the gazelle was that it was a delicacy served at Solomon's table (1 Kings 4:23). They are delicious to eat. They are fawn in color and when tamed are very affectionate.[7] Furthermore, they have a frolicksomeness and gaiety which irresistibly enchants the eyes of the beholder and attracts them to come near and touch them.[8] The lily is curvy and is often therefore alluded to as an architectural ornament.[9]

Casual reflections on the many associations connected with the words "gazelle" and "lilies" make his description of his wife's breast pregnant with beautiful connotations. They are very curvaceous like the lily. Their beauty creates within his heart a desire to reach out and fondle them as one would a gazelle feeding by a brook. The notion of frolicksomeness suggests sexual playfulness. The fact they were served as a delicacy to eat at Solomon's table suggests his desire to caress them with his lips and tongue. As gazelles were warm and affectionate, so was Shulamith as a sexual partner.

> 4:6   SOLOMON: Until the cool of the day
> When the shadows flee away,
> (at twilight time)
> I will go to the mountain of myrrh
> And to the hill of frankincense.

This appears to be synthetic parallelism. Thus the mountain of myrrh and the hill of frankincense are the same place. But what do they represent?

SOLOMON ON SEX

The female genitals are referred to in 5:1 as a "garden" and in 4:13 as "shoots" (see discussion on 4:13). In both passages, myrrh and frankincense are described as characteristic scents of her "garden."

Thus, when Solomon says he will go his way "to the mountain of myrrh," the reference to the *mountain* of myrrh and to the *hill* of frankincense becomes, in this interpretation, an obvious reference to the proverbial "Mount of Venus."

That this is the intent of the imagery is further reinforced by the fact that Solomon's praises and caresses start at her head and work downward. Note the sequence:

1. eyes—like doves
2. hair—long and black
3. teeth—white and smooth
4. lips—red and lovely
5. cheeks—red
6. neck—erect
7. breasts—full and youthful
8. "garden"—(mount of myrrh, etc.)—erotically scented

Solomon now sums up the beauty of his bride by saying:

4:7 SOLOMON: You are altogether beautiful my darling,
　　　　　　 And there is no blemish in you.

I once counseled a couple who were having some difficulties in the physical dimension of their marriage. The trouble, on the surface, seemed to be the wife's inhibitions. The husband was rather distraught at her refusal to disrobe and display her body to him.

The first question I asked him was, "Have you ever told your wife you thought her body was beautiful?"

She volunteered, "No he hasn't. I had no idea he thought my body was appealing to him. In fact, because he never expressed that it was appealing I sort of assumed it wasn't." As a result the inhibitions set in.

Every woman wants to believe her appearance arouses her man. Solomon is sensitive to this fact and expresses himself accordingly. Like any woman, Shulamith wanted to hear Solomon comment he liked what he saw when she entered the room.

The problem is, many women have "hang-ups" about various parts of their anatomy. They can stand in front of a mirror and see scores of imperfections that never even occurred to you. That appendectomy scar, for example, looks to her as if it's 18 inches long. If she has picked up a few stretch marks from having babies, as far as she is concerned her tummy looks like a plowed field. Her thighs are either too fat or too skinny. Her breasts are either too big, too small or too something.

Tell her she is beautiful to you. That's what Solomon is doing here and he's doing it in poetry!

Now there is a brief pause in their lovemaking while Solomon sums up her beauty in 4:7 and discusses a journey to the Lebanon mountains, her country home.

> 4:8 SOLOMON: Come with me from Lebanon, my bride,
> May you come with me from Lebanon.

The passage is somewhat difficult in view of the fact that they are in the bridal chamber in Jerusalem. Delitzsch argues that the Hebrew of the passage suggests he wants her *to go with him to* Lebanon up to the steep heights of the mountains.[10] He is promising her a vacation in the country. He will take her to the country home she loves. He describes what they will see and do while in the mountains:

> Journey down from the summit of Amana,

Amana is the name of one of the outermost peaks of the Lebanon mountains.

> From the summit of Senir and Hermon,

Hermon is the most southern peak of the Anti-libanus chain. This chain of mountains (about 10,000 feet) forms the northeastern border of Palestine. The springs of the Jordan River take their rise here. Senir is another section of the same mountain range. It is very probable that Solomon built royal residences in this region. It was his San Clemente and Camp David, a sort of northern White House. He is, in effect, promising her a vacation, or perhaps a honeymoon in the mountains north of where she was raised.

> From the dens of lions,
> From the mountains of leopards.

Leopards live in these mountains even today, although lions have long since become extinct. From the heights of these mountains, Solomon

SOLOMON ON SEX

promises they will honeymoon together and look down where the lions and leopards dwell.

Before moving on to verse 9, let's consider several principles related to sexual love that are evident in these verses. Put yourself in Shulamith's position. Two days earlier she had been walking around barefoot in the vineyards in the Lebanon mountains to the north. In the past forty-eight hours she had been transported south in a gala wedding procession, placed in the splendid palace of the richest man in the world, officiated at a wedding banquet, and now she finds herself alone with her new husband at last. That's quite a lot to happen to a country girl in two days!

Without a doubt she is probably a little restless inside. She probably is longing for her Lebanon home. She feels slightly out of place. Also, it seems evident she was somewhat concerned about her appearance in comparison to the lovely court ladies (1:5,6; 2:1,2), feeling she was only a "lily of the valley," a common country girl. In view of these inner feelings, Solomon's approach to lovemaking seems very exemplary.

In 4:8 he deals with her first concern—her longing for her country home. He promises her they will return there for the honeymoon.

Her second problem, her concern about her beauty, is dealt with in 4:1-7 where he tells her how beautiful she is. Solomon is a mind reader! He is very sensitive to his wife's psychological and emotional concerns and is not only concerned with his own satisfaction on the physical level.

Too frequently men tend to divorce sex from the total relationship. Women on the other hand tend to be so concerned about the relationship and the "spiritual" aspects of sex that to view it as pure pleasure and fun is offensive. Both extremes are wrong. Solomon is being extremely thoughtful and tender toward his new bride. A woman needs to feel her husband wants to make love to her as a person and not as a "body" or thing. Their loveplay here was relaxed, unrushed, and a time for enjoying one another as persons and not just as objects. Too many men carry a "thirty-second" approach into the bedroom and wonder why their wives never seem to be responsive. In order for sex to be an expression of love, the needs and desires of the other person should be more important than your own.

> Do nothing from selfish ambition or vain conceit, but in humility consider others better than yourselves. Each of you should look not only to your own interests, but also to the interests of others (Phil. 2:3-4).

If your lovemaking tends to last only five or ten minutes, you might consider whether or not you are really making love to your wife as a

THE WEDDING NIGHT

person or simply using her for a sexual release. Solomon's main concern was to satisfy his bride and not himself; as a result he received plenty of satisfaction in return (5:1).

After a brief interlude and joyful conversation, their lovemaking resumes at a faster pace in the following verses.

> 4:9 SOLOMON: You have made my heart beat faster, my sister,
> my bride.
> You have made my heart beat faster with a single
> glance of your eyes.

Her eyes were apparently very alluring and had the ability to arouse him.

> You have made my heart beat faster with a
> single strand of your necklace.
>
> 4:10 SOLOMON: How beautiful is your love, my sister, my bride,
> How much better is your love than wine,"

Solomon says her love ("caresses," see discussion on 1:2) are beautiful (2:3). They are more beautiful than wine, a symbol for supreme pleasure.[11]

When he says her love is better than wine, he is complimenting her on her love skill. She was a skillful mistress!

> And the fragrance of your oils
> Than all kinds of spices!

Her oils, those she naturally produces, are more fragrant to him than "all kinds of spices." Since the spices are also oils of myrrh, etc., the contrast must be between naturally produced "oils" (the moistness associated with feminine passion), and external man-made perfumes.

> 4:11 SOLOMON: Your lips, my bride, drip honey;
> Honey and milk are under your tongue,

These symbols speak of the sweetness of her kisses. "No doubt some historians of romance are under the illusion that a certain kind of kissing originated in France in recent centuries. This Song, however, was written long before that" one writer has noted.[12]

80

And the fragrance of your garments is
like the fragrance of Lebanon.

This apparently refers to a flimsy, scant, and perfumed negligee she is wearing while they are enjoying their love together. It must be sheer; he can see her breasts through it (4:5) and her "mountain of myrrh" (4:6). This attire provided Solomon with ample access to her feminine charms. Shulamith knew how to dress for bed!

One woman in a book I recently read put it this way: "Wives, if your husbands like black, see-through lingerie, don't wear flannel pajamas to bed. You're not living in a nunnery, you are sleeping with a man."[13] He's not interested in fighting through yards of cloth or "missionary mumus" in order to find you.

4:11 SOLOMON: A garden locked is my sister, my bride,
A rock-garden locked, a spring sealed up.

The garden refers to her vagina. When Solomon says it is locked, he is saying it has never been entered; she is a virgin.

Gardens and vineyards in Palestine were surrounded by rock walls to prevent intrusion of strangers. Only the lawful possessor of the garden could enter it.

Solomon's use of the word "garden" to describe his wife's genitals is full of poetic and symbolic beauty. The Hebrew word "gannah" is literally translated, "a covered or hidden place," and in the Eastern traveler's mind denotes much more than an ordinary garden does today. Gardens in biblical times "were usually walled inclosures, as the name indicates in which there were paths winding in and out among shade and fruit trees, canals of running water, fountains, sweet-smelling herbs, aromatic blossoms and convenient arbors in which to sit and enjoy the effect."[14]

The literature of ancient Egypt, Palestine, and Babylon indicates kings were especially fond of gardens and laid out vast expanses of rich gardens containing the rarest trees and plants. To the oriental mind, a garden was a place of shade and refreshment. Frequently the ancient picture of Paradise involves a shaded garden, the air laden with sweet perfumes from the fruits and flowers, accompanied by the music of running water and a couch upon which to recline. To the Hebrew mind, especially, the reference to a "garden" recalled the beauty and perfection of the Garden of Eden.

Only one who has traveled for days in a dry, glaring desert country (such as surrounds Palestine), and has come upon a beautiful shaded garden can appreciate how similar to Paradise these gardens can appear.

Thus to describe Shulamith's vagina as a garden is to say it is beautiful to behold, like flowered gardens of the East. It is also a source of sexual refreshment for him to experience. As a carefully cultivated Eastern garden yields delicious "fruit," so Shulamith's garden is a source of delicious fruit (sexual pleasures), when "cultivated." Furthermore, it is a source of fertility. To make love with her is like entering Paradise. Her pleasures are secret and hidden from all but Solomon—the rightful owner of the garden.

Not only does Solomon refer to her vagina as a "garden," but also as a "spring sealed up" (4:12). Because water was scarce in the East, owners of fountains sealed them with clay which quickly hardened in the sun. Thus, a sealed fountain was shut against all impurity; no one could get water out of it except its rightful owner.

Thus, Shulamith was closed against the world and inaccessible to all who would disturb her pure heart or desecrate her pure person.

4:13 SOLOMON: Your shoots are an orchard of pomegranates
With choice fruits, henna with nard plants,
4:14   Nard and saffron, calainus and cinnamon,
With all the trees of frankincense,
Myrrh and aloes, along with all the finest spices.

The Hebrew word translated "shoots" is used in the Old Testament to mean a missile or a weapon. It is also used of plants or fruit (Jer. 17:8; Ps. 80:12). Both meanings make no sense here. It seems Solomon is giving the word a distinct meaning unique to the love song. This should not be unexpected as he takes other common words and gives them erotic meanings ("oils," "garden," "fruit," etc.). Some of the commentators suggest the word should be translated "they sendings forth."[15] Although this interpretation has the advantage of being very literal, it lacks sense.

Perhaps Harris Hirschberg is correct when he says that since the preceeding verses are referring to the female anatomy, we should think of the Arabic "shalkh," or vagina.[16] Thus "the shoots" would refer to her "garden." This interpretation gains prominence in that the aroma of frankincense is attributed to her "shoots" in 4:14 and also to her "garden," or vagina, in 5:1. The plural, "shoots," is somewhat awkward in this interpretation, but it is probably a plural of intensity like *elohim* (God —Gods is a plural of intensity emphasizing the divine majesty). Zockler says the term "plants" refers to a single plant.[17]

By calling her "garden" an orchard of pomegranates, he says her garden contains the most delicious of fruits. Thus, he speaks of the pleasure awaiting him there.

The remainder of the verse refers to exotic, fragrant plants, most of which Solomon imported to Palestine. They constitute Solomon's erotic and poetic description of her "garden."

Nard is a fragrance-giving plant; saffron, a yellow plant; calainus, a plant of reedlike stem and tawny color which grows in wild marshes; cinnamon, a plant grown in the East Indies which grows to thirty feet in height.

The perfumed oil obtained from the myrrh plant is called myrrh and was used in gargles to scent the breath.[18] The ancients were very fond of sweet perfumes of all kinds, and perfumed oils were rubbed on the body and feet. Small pellets of dried mixed spice and resins or resinous woods were burned in special censers.[19] Perfume was used to scent the breath (Song 7:8). Clothing was perfumed (Ps. 45:8; Song 3:6; 4:11). Couches and beds were sprinkled (Prov. 7:17). Frankincense was sometimes chewed to give the mouth a fresh odor.[20] The aloes plant grows in India; its wood is very aromatic and was held in veneration by the natives.

The association of fragrant odor with the vagina is perplexing to many women. For various reasons many wives consider their genitals repulsive and cannot imagine how their husbands find them attractive. God created husbands to enjoy their wives' bodies, including the genitals. When the genitals have been thoroughly cleaned with soap and water, and when a woman is sexually aroused, there is a faint and very stimulating odor associated with the moistness. When he says her garden contains "the finest spices," he means it is as rare and as much to be valued as the most precious of aromatic herbs.

It is interesting again to see how some of the commentators avoid the obvious implications of Solomon's praises of the "scent" of her "garden." For example, Zockler in Lange's commentary says, "A particular explanation of the individual products of the garden is, on the whole, impossible, and leads to what is at variance with good taste."[21] But why is it "in variance with good taste" if God included it in Scripture and sanctioned it as beautiful and holy?

4:15 SOLOMON: You are a garden spring,
A well of fresh water,
And streams flowing from Lebanon.

THE WEDDING NIGHT

To him, she is not a sealed garden. Her garden is an open well from which he can draw refreshment as a tired and thirsty traveler could at a fountain. To what do the "streams flowing from Lebanon" refer? This phrase is used in Prov. 5:16 in a similar sexual context of male semen:

> Drink water from your own cistern
> And fresh water from your own well.

That is, have sexual intercourse only with your own wife;

> Should your springs be dispersed abroad,
> *Streams of water* in the streets?

McKane says, "It is the male semen which constitutes the 'springs' and channels of water. . ."[22]

> Let them be yours alone,
> And not for strangers with you.

". . . intercourse with a strange woman is a waste of semen, since it is the fathering of children from a strange household and a consequent neglect of the building up of one's own house and posterity."[23] McKane could have added that it is also immoral!

There seems to be a parallel thought here with Song 4:15; both passages are written by the same author, Solomon.

The wife in Prov.5:15, 16	*The husband in Prov.5:16*
waters out of a cistern	lest thy fountains by dispersed
running waters out of thine own well	rivers of water

If the "fountains" and waters of the male refer to his semen, then what do the rivers of waters of the wife refer to? As semen is the product of his sexual excitement, so running waters must be the product of hers. Thus, the running waters would refer to the juices which lubricate the vagina during intercourse. Since these streams were also a symbol of refreshment, the reference speaks of the sexual refreshment her garden provided.

It is worth noting she doesn't request sexual intercourse (4:16) until she is already well-lubricated. Too many husbands tend to start their lovemaking by direct genital stimulation, or they begin intercourse before the wife specifically indicates she is close to a climax and well lubricated. The mere fact that she is lubricated, however, does *not* mean she is ready for intercourse. Let her tell you when she's ready like Shulamith told Solomon.

> 4:16 SHULAMITH: Awake, O north wind
> And come, wind of the south.

She now responds to Solomon's praises. She calls him the north and south winds. The north wind brings clear weather and removes clouds, and the south brings warmth and moisture. When they blew across a garden in Palestine, coolness and sultriness, cold and heat, would promote the growth of the garden. She is asking Solomon to stimulate her garden with caresses to promote the growth of her sexual passion.

> Make my garden breathe out fragrance,
> Let its spices be wafted abroad.

As the "winds" blow through her garden, first from one direction and then from another, Shulamith's sexual passion grows and grows until all the fragrance of the garden rises in waves to become a sea of incense.[24] She wants everything in her which pleases her lover to show itself to him in full power and loveliness. As a traveler passed by an Eastern garden its scent would draw him to enter it. Shulamith wants her garden to become more and more "enticing" to Solomon as a result of his caresses. She wants a "sea of incense" to draw his interest to her garden until his passion is great! She completely accepts her femininity and is anxious that Solomon fully experience what she has to offer. She relishes the fact that Solomon is highly aroused by the sight of her garden and by caressing it. What a healthy attitude!

Now that she is fully aroused, she requests that Solomon enter her.

> 4:16 SHULAMITH: May my beloved come into his garden
> And eat its choice fruits!

> 5:1 SOLOMON: I have come into my garden, my sister,
> my bride
> I have gathered my myrrh along with
> my balsam.
> I have eaten my honeycomb and my honey;
> I have drunk my wine and my milk.

To gather, eat, and drink are all terms that speak of sexual enjoyment. Delitzsch says, "It supposes a union of love, such as is the conclusion of marriage following the bethrothal, the God-ordained aim of sexual love within the limits of morality."[25]

These references to wine and milk would be readily understood in that culture as fertility symbols.[26] Thus the poet sings of the mixture of his love with hers, of his semen with her vaginal moistness at the climax of their love.

After their love is consummated, a new speaker is introduced:

5:1 Eat, Friends,
   Drink and inbibe deeply, O lovers.

The commentators have differed widely on the identity of this speaker. The intimacies of the scene make consideration of a real human observer impossible. It cannot be the lovers who are speaking, for they are the ones being addressed.

The poet seems to say this is the voice of God Himself. Only the Lord could pronounce such an affirmation. He, of course, was the most intimate observer of all. Their love came from Him (Song 8:7). Thus, the Lord pronounces His full approval on everything that has taken place. He encourages them to drink deeply of the gift of sexual love.

There is a beautiful unity to this chapter. It opens with Solomon's praise and his concern for the emotional state of his bride (4:1–7). Their loveplay pauses while he promises her a honeymoon in the Lebanon mountains to the north (4:8). They then resume their love play and his heart beats faster and faster (4:9–11). He begins to caress her garden and stimulate her passion (4:12–15). She then invites him to enter her (4:16); they consummate their love (5:1), and the Lord pronounces His approval on everything that has taken place.

COMMENT

Bedroom language

Notice the very erotic and sensual language they use to stimulate each other as they are making love. She speaks of the spices of her garden being wafted abroad. She asks him to eat of her garden's fruit. He calls her vagina a fruit orchard and describes her vaginal moistness as streams flowing from Lebanon (her home town). His genitals are called "fruit" in Song 2:3 and hers a "garden" in 4:12–16. The song has dealt very delicately with some extremely erotic and personal subjects, and yet one can read it and not take offense.

Robert Gordis discusses the value of poetic symbolism in subjects like this very well.

> It is characteristic of the delicacy of the songs that the woman in each case expresses her desire for love by indirection. While a blunt avowal would repel by its crassness, the use of symbolism, which conceals as it reveals, heightens by its subtlety the charm of the sentiments expressed. Psycho-analytic theory has offered a highly plausible explanation for this powerful appeal of symbolism to the human spirit.
>
> According to psychoanalysis the unconscious persistently seeks some avenue of expression which will elude the 'censor' who stands guard over the conscious mind. Symbolism performs this liberating function for the unconscious admirably, because, in its very nature, it expresses far more than it says; its nuances are at best as significant as its explications. Its overt meaning has nothing in it to arouse the vigilance of the censor, and meanwhile its deeper context is able to cross the threshold of consciousness.[27]

In translating the symbolism, one risks the danger of appearing crass. This is the ever-present danger in this book! When God spoke of personal aspects of sex, He could have used the slang terms; however, they would tend to raise up that psychological censor. He could have used the medical terms, but that leaves a feeling of "mechanics" and science and often a sense of awkwardness.

The Lord avoided both problems by using poetic symbolism. It is impossible, however, for the interpreter of the Song to leave it in poetry; to do so leaves it without interpretation to modern readers unfamiliar with ancient oriental symbols. It is the job of a commentator to explain the symbols just as an expositor of the book of Revelation must do.

On "dressing up" for your mate

While it is certainly true that God looks on the heart, and that the focus on clothes and appearance can be overdone, it is also true that the letters M-R-S (Mrs.) before your name do not stand for Miserable Rut of Sloppiness, or Miss Rummage Sale. But judging from the looks of the typical housewife, you would never know it.

Take a look at nine out of ten women pushing carts in a supermarket. They look like survivors of a shipwreck wearing clothes distributed by the Red Cross. They spend more time selecting a head of cabbage than a new shade of lipstick.

The next time you go shopping, count the number of women you feel the average man would find sexy. The aisles of a supermarket offer a horrifying potpourri of feminine ugliness. The 'Girl Scout Leader' types with their pulled-back run-a-quick-comb-through-it hair and hem lines that are never quite right. The 'good mother' types with their cracked fingernails and broken-zippered Bermudas (hair forever in plastic curlers).[28]

Ask yourself this question, ladies: "Would I have wanted him to see me looking this way before we were married?" If you cannot answer yes, you need to make some changes. When your husband leaves for work, he carries a picture of you in his mind. Is that image likely to give him romantic thoughts during his afternoon coffee break? Solomon says the image of the Shulamite left these kinds of thoughts in his mind!

It seems strange that wives and husbands often save their best for comparative strangers while their mate must settle for what he (she) can get. After you collapse on the couch completely "exhausted" from a "hard day," he's supposed to understand, right? He ought to; you have explained it to him in tiresome detail. Yet let an insurance salesman or a friend drop by, and instantly you become all smiles, coffee, and conversation.

What do you look like when he comes home from work? Do you get the house ready, and more importantly do you get yourself ready?

A man needs a "magnet" at home that keeps drawing him back. If he does not find that magnet at home, there are hundreds of them out in the business world. The girls at the office always appear to him at their best!

The way Shulamith dresses has a definite effect on her sex appeal to her husband. Note in 4:11 where Solomon comments on the "fragrance of her garments." She is skilled in the use of perfumes and cosmetics which make her as attractive to her husband as possible (see 1:9,10,15; 4:1–7; 6:4–9; 7:1–7).

These comments need some qualification. No woman should be expected to appear as if she stepped out of a beauty parlor twenty-four hours a day. The home should be a place where one can relax and "let your hair down." All we are suggesting is that often we let too much hair down and the result is very thoughtless.

Men are no less guilty of sloppiness than many women. Too many husbands lay around the house in sweatshirts or dirty work clothes. They

SOLOMON ON SEX

lounge in front of the TV set watching football with their overweight bellies hanging over their belts and wonder why their wives are not sexually responsive to them.

Do you make her feel needed?

Solomon did! When he gazed at her body and referred to the stately carriage of her neck (4:4), he was poetically telling her, "My darling, you are a constant source of encouragement and strength for me. I need you desperately to carry out my responsibilities as King of Israel."

Have you ever told your wife something like that? She needs to feel needed. You also need to feel needed. If your boss continually communicated to you that you were unnecessary to the function of the company, your motivations to do a good job would rapidly disappear. You and the family are her world. She needs to know she's succeeding at her "job" just as much as you need that assurance on yours.

The problem is she often has a difficult time trying to determine exactly what you need her for. She pleasures you in bed, takes care of your things, keeps the place attractive for you and sees that there are three meals on the table every day.

But what else? She wants to know how much you appreciate her encouragement. Tell her what her support does to give you the incentive to go on. Tell her you need to know she believes in you, trusts you, and has faith in you. She needs to know you recognize that need and rely on her faith.

President Ford in his acceptance speech said, "I am indebted to no man and to only one woman." He was telling the world she contributed to his success. He was giving her honor (1 Pet. 3:7).

If it is difficult for you to express this to her, work on your inhibitions; you might try writing it all out in loving detail and sending it to her in a special delivery letter! She may tend to evaluate herself in terms of dishwashing, floor scrubbing, and all those other "busy" chores. And believe me, it isn't these things that make her feel important in your life!

The biblical definition of "romance"

Women are incurable romantics with no discernable interest in being cured. If you ever wrote her any love letters, chances are she has kept every one of them. Men are harmed by a lack of romantic love to a much less degree than women, and we men therefore cannot appreciate its importance to her. If a man is denied this, he generally throws himself into his work and finds fulfillment there. Not so a woman; since her life is more directly focused in the home she probably feels this lack more deeply than a man.

A man once told his wife on their wedding day, "I want you to know I love you. If I didn't I wouldn't have married you. I expect to continue to love you, but don't expect me to say any more about it. Remember, I have already said it."

The wife was speechless and, guided by instinct, said, "Oh, I can't remember something like that. I think you will have to remind me again and again." As plants need sunshine and water, so a woman needs romantic love if she is to flourish and bloom.[29]

In chapter 4 we see a beautiful illustration of romantic love. In fact, the whole book illustrates this point and defines it for us in tangible ways. Many women complain that their husbands are not romantic enough, but they never seem to be able to define exactly this mysterious substance called "romance." Listen carefully, men; you are at last going to get a definition, and from the Bible, no less! The Song of Solomon seems to teach that "romance" has at least four ingredients.

(1) *It includes an element of the unexpected*. When Solomon constructs a bedroom with cedars from Lebanon (1:16,17) to surprise his bride, he's being romantic. When he springs a surprise vacation in the Lebanon mountains on her, he's being romantic. The element of surprise is important to romance. A single long-stemmed rose when there is no special occasion is romantic.

Anything that repeats itself over and over again loses its romantic value, such as always having dinner at the same restaurant, with movies always to follow.

(2) *It includes dating*. We find Solomon taking his wife-to-be on a date in 2:8-17. After they are married, he still takes her on dates (7:11-8:14). Do you regularly date your wife like Solomon did?

Let me carefully define what I do not mean by a "date." It is not hurling a newspaper her way some evening while you are laying in front of a boring TV show and saying, "Honey, why don't you see if there is anything on at the movies and call and get a babysitter?"

A date is when *you* plan the evening, *you* get the babysitter, and YOU TAKE HER. You remember, like you did *before* you married her. You might get a list of the names and phone numbers of all the babysitters she uses. Something is missing if you have to ask her where to go. When you

SOLOMON ON SEX

were dating her before you married her, you didn't wait for her to come up with the ideas.

Also, a date is one husband and one wife, not a crowd. Double dates went out with the junior prom. Going out with another couple is great; do it often, but that's not a date.

Generally, what happens is that you spend the evening talking to him, and your wife spends the evening talking to her, and a week later she says, "Why don't you ever take me out?"

You reply, "I just took you out last week!"

But you didn't take *her* out. You were "out" with the other wife's husband! Call going out with another couple "Christian fellowship" or something . . . but that's not what we're talking about when we speak of a "date."

Sometimes your dates should involve pre-planning that appears spontaneous. For example, let's say you are going window-shopping with your wife on an evening downtown. You casually pass by a restaurant and say, "Why don't we go in and get a bite to eat."

When you enter the restaurant, there are twenty-five people waiting to be seated, and the waiter informs you it will be about an hour and a half before you can get a table.

Just at that moment the head waiter arrives and says, "Good evening, Mr. Jones, we have your table for two right over here overlooking the lights of the city." That's romance! That's pre-planning that appears spontaneous.

What can you do on a date? Here are some suggestions:

—Take a window-shopping stroll *after* the stores have closed.
—Go river bank fishing by moonlight without too much attention to fishing.
—Find a secluded spot and build a fire.
—Go for a drive in the car and just talk.
—Go bicycling.
—Go ice or roller skating.
—Visit a zoo.
—Visit the airport (you might even "watch the airplanes" like you did before you married her).
—Go on a camp-out.
—Go to a rodeo.
—Visit a museum.
—Visit a library some evening and browse through all the books on sex, love, and marriage.

91

THE WEDDING NIGHT

—Spend an evening sharing mutual goals and planning family objectives.

—Locate an unusual and different restaurant and spend the evening there in loving conversation.

—Spend an evening making love in a motel, away from the children and the phone. Be home by midnight.

—Go to the drive-in.

—Visit a convalescent home and take some presents to cheer up the patients and elderly people.

(3) *It includes the impractical*. Cedars from Lebanon are very impractical for bedroom construction! Furthermore, kings can't afford time frivolously spent wandering through the forests of Lebanon mountains with their wives (7:11). How impractical! Our emphasis of "being practical" is a major killer of romance. There is a beautiful illustration of impracticality in the Old Testament.

David and his mighty men were at war with the Philistines. One day David casually remarked that he desired a drink of water out of the well of Bethlehem (1 Sam. 23:13-17). The problem was this well was now located behind enemy lines and in the middle of the Philistine camp!

Three of David's "Five Star Generals," the chiefs of the mighty men, overheard his remark. That night they crept away from the camp and secretly crossed enemy lines and crept right into the Philistine campsite. After securing a pitcher of water from the well, they returned to the Israelite camp completely undetected.

When they gave their gift to David, he was so overwhelmed that he said, "I am not worthy to drink this water," and he poured it out on an altar as a sacrifice to the Lord.

What utter nonsense! The three top men in David's army risk their own lives and therefore the future of David's military operations against the Philistines for a pitcher of water! It may be impractical nonsense, but it is this kind of nonsense that makes the world go around.

Creative romantic love is often stifled by the desire to be reasonable and practical. "This isn't a strategic way to spend money."

"We're too old for that sort of thing."

"Why don't we wait until we have fulfilled all of these other responsibilities."

I'm not advocating irresponsibility. I'm simply observing that practicality can sometimes squelch love. Don't hesitate to be impractical once in a while.

Your wife may need an ironing board to the point of desperation. That would be a very "practical" gift but it rates quite low in the romance department.

When I was a child I always bought my mother practical gifts for Christmas like knives, plates, placemats, etc. Those gifts are necessary, but we are supposed to be men now.

Buy her some perfume, scented soap, a record, lingerie, a basket of fruit, a new plant for the house, or the new outfit she wanted but couldn't afford.

(4) *It includes creativity.* Solomon is a very creative lover. We find this illustrated profusely throughout the Song. It takes creativity to design that kind of bedroom (1:16,17); he speaks to her in poetry to describe her beauty (4:1–7); he takes her for walks in the forests and they make love outdoors (7:11–13); he buys her little trinkets and pieces of jewelry (1:11); he encourages variety in their loveplay (7:1–11).

How creative are you toward your wife? Men tend to think in categories and settle down into the rut of marriage very quickly. We use a systematic and categorized approach to our jobs and unfortunately often carry it over into our relationships with our wives.

I once talked to a woman who told me of her husband's lovemaking: "I can tell you exactly what my husband will do next, how long he will linger on that part of my body to the second. He hasn't changed the routine in twenty years." She doesn't want a tired old man who treats her to a "good-old-reliable-mother-to-my-children" kind of affection.

It has been said the only difference between a rut and a grave is the depth of it. If you have fallen into that nine-to-five, sex-only-after-the-late-news, camping-vacations-*always*-with-the-children-along rut, don't expect her to be a very exciting lover. Introduce creativity into your lovemaking and your total relationship like Solomon did.

To find out just how creative you are as a husband, may I suggest you take the following "Lover's Quotient Test." Give yourself ten points for each item on the following list if you have done it once in the past six months. If you have done any item on the list two or more times, you get twenty points.

—Have you phoned her during the week and asked her out for one evening that weekend without telling her where you are taking her? A mystery date.
—Have you given her an evening completely off? You clean up the kitchen; you put the kids to bed.
—Have you gone parking with her at some *safe* and secluded spot and

kissed and talked for an evening?

—Have you drawn a bath for her after dinner? Put a scented candle in the bathroom; add bath oil to the bath; send her there right after dinner, and then you clean up and put the kids to bed while she relaxes. (My wife says in order to get any points for this you you must also clean up the tub!)

—Have you phoned her from work to tell her you were thinking nice thoughts about her? (You get no points for this one if you asked what was in the mail.)

—Have you written her a love letter and sent it special delivery? (First class mail will do.)

—Have you made a tape recording of all the reasons you have for loving her? Give it to her wrapped in a sheer negligee!

—Have you given her a day off? Send her out to do what she wants. You clean the house, fix the meals, and take care of the kids. (My wife says you ought to get thirty points for this one.)

—Have you put a special effect stereo recording of ocean waves on tape and played it while you had a nude luau on the living room floor? (If this seems a little far out for your tastes, you could substitute by either removing the stereo effects tape or having a popcorn party in the privacy of the bedroom.)

—Have you spent a whole evening (more than two hours) sharing mutual goals and planning family objectives with her and the children?

—Have you ever planned a surprise weekend? You make the reservations and arrange for someone to keep the children for two days. Tell her to pack her suitcase, but don't tell her where you are going. (Just be sure it's not the Super Bowl.) Make it someplace romantic.

—Have you picked up your clothes just one time in the past six months and put them on hangers?

—Have you given her an all-over body massage with scented lotion and a vibrator?

—Have you spent a session of making love to her that included at least two hours of romantic conversation, shared dreams, many positions of intercourse, and much variety of approach and caresses?

—Have you repaired something around the house which she has not requested?

—Have you kissed her passionately for at least thirty seconds one morning just before you left for work, or one evening when you walked in the door?

—Have you brought her an unexpected little gift like perfume, a ring, or an item of clothing?

—Have you replaced her old negligee?

I have given this ridiculous test to men all over the country. Let's see how your scores compare with theirs.

200-360—LOVER— You undoubtably have one of the most satisfied wives in the country.

150-200—GOOD— Very few make this category.

100-150—AVERAGE—This husband is somewhat typical and usually not very exciting as a lover.

50-100—KLUTZ— Too many score in this category. I hope you'll begin to move up soon.

0- 50—HUSBAND— There is a difference between a "husband" and a "lover." The only reason your wife is still married to you is that she's a Christian; she has unusual capacity for unconditional acceptance, and there are some verses in the Bible against divorce.

While the test shouldn't be taken too seriously, it does outline a plan of attack to increase your creativity level. I realize that many things on the list may not fit your temperament and your marriage relationship. *Make up your own list.* The idea is simply to encourage creativity in a fun way.

After giving this test as a humorous conclusion to messages on sex for men, I find varied reactions. Most of the men seem to like it and leave encouraged to break the routine of the marriage. One man wrote me and said the whole thing was silly and ridiculous! Furthermore, *everyone* he had talked to agreed.

This test may be ridiculous as far as its application to your marriage relationship is concerned. Fine. Furthermore, there are many sincere, godly men who are very creative in their approach to their wives, but who scored poorly on the test. The issue is what is appropriate in your particular and unique marriage relationship that will bring new zest and vitality.

At the conclusion of one seminar, a man rated in the lover category. He had a score of 340! Another man on the front row laughed out loud when he heard the score and blurted, "How long has he been married?" He was implying that the man who scored so highly must have been only recently married. Once you settle down in the daily routine and have been married for a number of years, he reasoned, these things are no longer expected as a regular part of married life; they are for "young couples."

If you are responding this way, let me ask you a question. Does your relationship with the Lord Jesus become more and more "settled" with time? Does it automatically lose its creativity and zest the longer you know Him? If it does, then you have a definite spiritual problem in your relationship with Him. It is not growing.

The Bible says the believer's relationship to Christ is to illustrate the husband's relationship to his wife physically. Just as a lack of spiritual vitality reflects a spiritual problem, a lack of growth in the vitality of your marriage relationship reveals a marriage problem. If your marriage is truly an illustration of Christ and the church, it should become more and more vital, free, and exciting as the years go by.

The other side of this is, of course, creativity as a wife. We will pick up some suggestions in that area when we discuss Song 7:13 in another chapter. For now, this brings the first part of the Song to a close. We must now turn our attention to the second half, in which we glean insight into resolving marital problems.

FOOTNOTES

1. Franz Delitzsch, *Commentary on the Song of Solomon and Ecclesiastes* (Grand Rapids: Eerdmans, n.d.), p. 71.
2. Rabbi Dr. S. M. Lehrman, *The Song of Songs, The Five Megilloth* ed. Dr. A. Cohen (The Soncino Press, 1946), p. 13.
Also Jameison, Fausset, & Brown, *Commentary on the Old and New Testaments* (5 vols; Grand Rapids: Eerdmans, 1967), III, p. 553.
3. Lehrman, p. 14.
4. Delitzsch, p. 76.
5. Dr. Otto Zockler, *The Song of Songs, Lange's Commentary* (Grand Rapids: Zondervan, 1960), Vol. 5, p. 63.
6. *International Standard Bible Encyclopedia (ISBE)*, ed. James Orr (5 vols; Grand Rapids: Eerdmans, 1939), II, p. 1179.
7. *Hastings Dictionary of the Bible*, ed. James Hastings (5 Vols; T&T Clark, 1904), II, 116.
8. Zockler, V, 86.
9. Hastings, III, 122.
10. Delitzsch, p. 79.
11. ISBE, V, 3089.
12. S. Craig Glickman, *A Song for Lovers* (Downers Grove: InterVarsity Press, 1976), p. 20.

SOLOMON ON SEX

13. Lois Bird, *How to be a Happily Married Mistress* (Garden City: Doubleday & Company, Inc., 1974).

14. ISBE, II, 1174.

15. Lehrman, p. 16.

16. *Vestus Testamentum*, No. 4 (Sept. 1961), p. 380.

17. Zockler, V, 89.

18. *Hasting's Dictionary of the Bible*, III, 749.

19. ISBE, 2102.

20. *Hasting's Dictionary of the Bible,* III, p. 747.

21. Zockler, V, 89.

22. William McKane, *Proverbs* in *The Old Testament Library* (Philadelphia: Westminster Press, 1970), p. 319.

23. Ibid., p. 318.

24. Zockler, V, 90.

25. Delitzsch, p. 88.

26. F. Delitzsch, *The Book of Job* (2 vols.; Grand Rapids: Eerdmans, 1949), I, 167. "The sperma is likened to milk." cf. Job 10:10.

27. Robert Gordis, *The Song of Songs* (New York: The Jewish Theological Seminary of America, 1954), p. 38.

28. Bird, p. 74.

29. Aubrey P. Andelin, *Man of Steel and Velvet* (Santa Barbara: Pacific Press, 1972), p. 235.

CHAPTER SEVEN
A DREAM OF LOVE
REFUSED—A PROBLEM

(Reflection #9, Song 5:2 –8)

Let's review the first part of the book for a moment. From 1:1 to 5:1, Shulamith's reflections deal with the wedding day and the wedding night. These chapters portray the ideal—the beauties of youthful and romantic love. Now, in the second major section of the book, a series of seven reflections portray the reality of married love. There are problems and adjustments that must be made if two people are to learn to live together in a vital marriage. The Bible is quite realistic; it doesn't leave us with an idealized picture of them living happily ever after.

There were two major problems that affected the early years of this marriage. The first concerned some problems related to sex. Solomon's job apparently kept him away from Shulamith more than she liked, and he was in the habit of approaching her sexually late at night after she was already in bed. She, in turn, continually displayed a lack of interest in sex and often rejected his advances.

The second problem surfaces in chapter six. Shulamith is a country girl at heart. She longs for the freedom of the country. Even though she loves Solomon, she would still like to visit her country home in the Lebanon mountains. The first part of this section of the book (5:2–8:4) reveals how they resolved their sexual differences. The second part gives the solution to the longing of Shulamith's heart, a vacation to the Lebanon mountains (8:5–13).

The first part of this section consists of five reflections. It begins with "A Dream of Love Refused" (5:2–8) and ends with "The Dance of the Mahanaim" (6:13b–8:4). It can be diagrammatically set forth like this:

From "A Dream of Love's Refusal" to "The Dance of the Mahanaim"
(Song 5:2–8:4)

THE PROBLEM: LOVE REFUSED	THE SOLUTION: ASSUMING PERSONAL RESPONSIBILITY				
A Dream of Love Refused	A Change of Attitude		A Thoughtful Interlude		A Change of Action
	My Beloved and My Friend		The Return of Solomon	Shulamith in the Garden	The Dance of the Mahanaim
"I have taken off my dress, how can I put it on again?" (5:3)	Concerning: thinking about sex What kind of beloved is your beloved?	Concerning: her husband's availability. Where has your beloved gone?	"You are as beautiful as Tirzah, my darling." (6:4)	"Come back come back, O Shulammite" (6:13a)	
5:2 8	9 16	6:1 3	4 10	11 13a	13b 8:4

The section begins with her passive apathy toward her husband's late-night advances and ends (after a decisive change of attitude, 5:9–6:3) with her active aggressiveness in initiating sexual play

(6:13b–8:4). The problem is sexual adjustment and many pertinent applications are suggested by this chapter to twentieth century marriage.

This song opens with Shulamith in a semi-conscious dream state. She is troubled and restless; her "heart is awake." Sometimes a restless dream of an unpleasant event reflects a degree of inner distress concerning the event. Many have found themselves dreaming about things that upset them during the day or about a particularly disturbing problem they are facing. The poet may have included the dream as a way of telling his readers that the problem troubling Shulamith is very upsetting to her. Insofar as the dream seems to contain a scene in which she is being punished (beaten by the palace guards) perhaps we are to assume she was feeling guilt over ignoring Solomon's sexual interest.

COMMENTARY

5:2 SHULAMITH: I was asleep, but my heart was awake.

To sleep while the heart is awake is to dream. The Hebrew text reads more literally, "I sleep and my heart keeps on waking." It was a restless and dream-filled night for Shulamith. She evidently tossed throughout the night in a restless sleep, stirring oft-times in a troublesome dream.

This section of the Song reveals two possible causes for her restless night. First of all, she and the king have had difficulties resolving some sexual problems (5:2,3). Secondly, she seems to have developed a longing for life in the country once again, and she has had trouble fully adjusting to palace life (6:12,13; 7:12).

The sexual problems are the focus of attention in the dream. A person only keeps on dreaming and has a restless night if there is a recurrent problem underlying the dream. In this case she seems to be upset with herself for her refusal of Solomon's late-night approach to sex. He had approached her after she was already in bed, and she had refused him; apparently she feels guilty about it. In the fantasy of her dreams, she imagines that she refused him, and after he left she could never find him.

5:2 SHULAMITH: A voice! My beloved was knocking:
Open to me, my sister, my darling,
My dove, my perfect one!
For my head is drenched with dew,
My locks with the damp of the night.

SOLOMON ON SEX

During some months in Palestine, dew falls so copiously that it saturates the clothes like rain (Judges 5:38). Solomon, apparently at an affair of state, comes to her bedroom in the dream and asks to make love. We know it is late at night because the dew has already begun to fall.

It could be that in the dream she is thinking of herself as back at her country home. This at least makes the reference to dew and the opening in the window (5:4) easier to explain. But dreams are very subtle, and not too much should be made of this. As she dreams the scene shifts back to the streets of Jerusalem—an impossibility, of course, in real life.

Now she gives two reasons why she is not interested in making love.

5:3 SHULAMITH: I have taken off my dress,
How can I put it on again?

If this seems like a strange reason to you for not making love, it seems strange to me also. She says she would have to put her robe on, get up and walk to the door, and open it. In effect, she's saying something like, "Oh Solomon, can't it wait? Can't you see that I'm tired and in bed?"

Then she gives her second excuse. This time she gets religious about it.

I have washed my feet,
How can I dirty them again?

The soiling of the feet was counted as a symbol of moral contamination from the petty transgressions of everyday life (John 13:10). They would often wash their feet ceremonially at night to symbolize their need for daily cleansing from sin, just as Jesus illustrated to His disciples (John 13:10).[1]

She is saying, "If I get up to let you in to make love, I'll get my feet dirty walking across the floor. Then I would have to wash them again before I could go back to bed."

Now both of these statements are obviously excuses! "I'll have to put my bathrobe on, and I'll get my feet dirty!" What she is trying to convey to her late-night lover is that she's tired, already in bed, and just not in the mood. The dew suggests it's pretty late at night, about the time of the conclusion of "The Late Show" on TV.

Shulamith now awakens thoroughly and finally begins to respond to Solomon's interests.

A DREAM OF LOVE REFUSED

5:4 SHULAMITH: My beloved extended his hand through
              the opening,
              And my feelings were aroused for him.

It was the ancient custom to secure the door of a house by a cross bar or
by a bolt, which at night was fastened with a little button or pin.[2] In the
upper part of the door, there was a round hole through which any person
from the outside might thrust his arm and remove the bar, unless the hole
was sealed up. As Shulamith saw Solomon's hand, she realized his desire
for her, and she had guilt feelings about her lack of availability. Then she
decided Solomon didn't have such a bad idea after all, and "her feelings
were aroused for him."

5:5 SHULAMITH: I arose to open to my beloved;
              And my hand dripped with myrrh,
              And my fingers with liquid myrrh,
              On the handles of the bolt.

In the fantasy of the dream, she associates her husband's approaches
toward her sexually with scented lotions. In their culture, a lover would
leave this fragrant myrrh at the door as a sign he had been there.[3]

5:6 SHULAMITH: I opened to my beloved
              But my beloved had turned away and had gone!
              My heart went out to him . . . but I did not
                 find him;
              I called him, but he did not answer me.

In her dream she is grieved to see Solomon has left. He had come to
make love (an inappropriate time, his fault); she refused him (her fault),
and now he has left with wounded pride. There is nothing more deflating
to a person's ego than to have one's mate continually reject his or her
sexual advances.
  Her discovery that her husband has left compounds her guilt, and she
now imagines that as she searches for him, the watchmen punish her.

5:7 SHULAMITH: The watchmen who make the rounds in the city
              found me,
              They struck me and wounded me;
              The guardsmen of the walls took away my
                 shawl from me.

SOLOMON ON SEX

As Shulamith dreams, she fancies herself out in the streets of Jerusalem searching for Solomon after refusing him. Obviously, the watchmen would not in reality lay a hand on Solomon's queen, but this is a dream. The fact that the guards beat her may indicate she is plagued with guilt because of her rejection of Solomon.

5:8 SHULAMITH: I adjure you, O daughters of Jerusalem,
     If you find my beloved,
     As to what to tell him:
     For I am lovesick.

The exact chronology of this dream sequence is difficult to follow. There seems to be no definite agreement among commentators as to when the dream ends and reality resumes. It appears to me, however, that due to the shift in tone and personal address in 5:8, the dream is over and a new scene is introduced. The chorus and the Shulamite girl have a conversation pinpointing the implications of the dream and some keys to solving their problems.

Others say the dream continues all the way to 6:3. It makes little difference, however, to our understanding of the main thrust of the poet's message. Thus, 5:8 could either be viewed as the conclusion of the dream (inserted by the poet to make a transition to the next scene), or as the introductory verse to the following scene.

She addresses the imaginary, non-existent chorus, instructing them to help her locate Solomon and tell him she is "lovesick." This is the same word used in 2:5, and it carries the notion of being highly aroused sexually.

The dream has now ended, but the powerful feeling of repentance and separation the dream left behind causes Shulamith to awaken, observe that Solomon is not beside her, and seek the aid of the chorus in finding him. The effects of the dream were so strong she remembers it as an actual experience.

Apparently, the dream has set her desires in motion, for she awakens "lovesick." The chorus is to tell Solomon that Shulamith deeply desires to make love with him. This would obviously be inappropriate if the daughters of Jerusalem really existed. In this case, this literary device enables Shulamith to express herself when no one is there.

As she awakes, she realizes her husband is away on affairs of state (Song 6:2-3). This causes her to reflect on the understanding she had before she married Solomon. She had counted the cost before they were

A DREAM OF LOVE REFUSED

married and had anticipated that separation could be a problem; she was not caught by surprise.

Instead of reacting with bitterness or resentment, she designed a creative alternative that would meet her needs as well as Solomon's within the framework of life they had chosen. That alternative partly involved periodic vacations in the country (7:11).

It seems apparent there is an intentional contrast with the dream of 3:1–4. In both dreams, Shulamith seeks her husband (3:3; 5:7).

The first dream is just before the wedding night, and the second dream is just after it.

In the first, she seeks her husband and finds him. In Chapter 5:2–8, she searches only to be beaten by the night watchmen.

In the dream of separation, we find Shulamith longing for her husband; in the dream of love refused, the emphasis is on taking her husband's sexual interest for granted. This contrast serves to heighten the import of her rejection.

COMMENT

These passages illustrate that sexual adjustment is not automatic. Too often young married couples think they will get married and fall into bed and immediately experience a beautiful sexual relationship. The Bible realistically portrays that such is not always the case. One study revealed that marriage failures due to sexual problems could be as high as 75 to 80 percent.[4]

Several common problems relating to sexual adjustment in marriage are suggested here.

Rejection

The following letter is written in jest, humorously exposing the issue of rejection.

"To My Loving Wife"

During the past year I have tried to make love to you 365 times. I have succeeded only 36 times; this is an average of once every 10 days. The following is a list of why I did not succeed more often.

It will wake the children .... 27 times
It's too late .... 23 times
It's too hot .... 16 times

It's too cold	5 times
It's too early	15 times
Pretended to be asleep	46 times
Windows open, neighbors will hear	9 times
Backache	26 times
Headache	18 times
Toothache	13 times
Giggles	6 times
Not in the mood	36 times
Too full	10 times
Baby is crying	17 times
Watched late TV show	17 times
I watched late TV show	15 times
Mud Pack	11 times
Company in next room	11 times
You had to go to the bathroom	19 times
TOTAL	**329 times**

During the 36 times I did succeed, the activity was not entirely satisfactory due to the following:

1. Six times you chewed gum during the whole time.
2. Seven times you watched TV the whole time.
3. Sixteen times you told me to hurry up and get it over with.
4. Six times I tried to wake you to tell you we were through.
5. One time I was afraid I had hurt you for I felt you move.

Honey, it's no wonder I'm so irritable!

YOUR LOVING HUSBAND

This letter reveals that "rejection" can be both physical and psychological. It is just as much a rejection of your mate to seem passively uninvolved as it is to actively reject. I read of one lady who gives her husband a check list of things she wants done around the house every Saturday morning. If he does everything on the list, he gets a "reward" Saturday night. Talk about rejection! That is psychological rejection.

Note the command of Scripture:

The husband should fulfill his marital duty to his wife, and likewise the wife to her husband. The wife's body does not belong to her alone but also to her husband. In the same way, the husband's body does not belong to him alone but also to his wife. Do not deprive each other except by mutual consent and for a time, so that you may devote yourselves to prayer. Then come together again so that Satan will not tempt you because of your lack of self-control. (1 Cor. 7:3–5)

A DREAM OF LOVE REFUSED

The Word here is quite strong. It is sin to reject your mate's sexual interests (actively or passively). This may seem harsh, but extensive counseling in numerous situations have borne this out in my experience. I have heard some of the most involved and sincere reasons for rejecting one's mate physically, but when we eventually got to the root of it, there was generally a problem of selfishness and sin somewhere.

This passage gives only three conditions lawful under God for a married couple to abstain from regular sexual relations.

(1) When there has been mutual consent,
(2) When it is only for a short period of time, and
(3) When the purpose is to devote oneself to prayer.

In the above letter, numerous excuses were offered for rejection, but prayer wasn't on the list. I don't know of anyone who has offered *that* reason to his mate!

In this passage, Shulamith rejects her husband, but the reverse situation is also common. The notion that men are always the ones interested in sex and women simply don't have as great a need is not well-supported by recent studies. Miles, in a survey of 150 Christian couples, asked, "How often would you like to have intercourse and orgasms if you could have this experience every time you really wanted to?" The husbands replied they would like it every 2.7 days (average), and the wives every 3.2 days.[5]

Thus, there is virtually no difference revealed in this particular study. In fact, up until the modern era, it was women who were considered to have the greater sexual appetites.[6] It is interesting that throughout the Song of Solomon and in 1 Cor. 7 there seems to be an underlying assumption that there is no real difference in the sexual needs or drives between men and women. As far as the Bible speaks to the issue, a woman's need is viewed as equal to a man's.

There are significant differences in psychological outlook, timing, and other factors, but the capacity and desire for sex is equal.

Shulamith's rejection of Solomon raises the question of "normal" frequency.

One woman sputtered with defiant frustration to a counselor, "Why my husband is so oversexed he would insist on making love to me at least twice a month if I'd let him!"

The couples Miles interviewed revealed they enjoyed intercourse to orgasm an average of 3.3 times per week. However, these statistics are really quite meaningless to a specific couple's situation. The issue is what is appropriate for your unique relationship and not some "national average."

Based on 1 Cor. 7:3-5, Shirley Rice gives three dangers of rejecting your mate's sexual initiatives.

(1) Your fellowship with the Lord is in jeopardy because it is a sin to violate a command of Scripture.
(2) Your relationship with your mate can be damaged or ruined.
(3) You will perhaps tempt your mate to adultery through the resulting anger and frustration.[8]

One reason so many men appear to be obsessed with sex is because they get so little of it from their wives. If a man hasn't eaten in five days, every time he passes the refrigerator food is all he can think about. Like food, sex isn't the most important thing in life; but if you are not totally available, it can become an obsession to your husband.

The reason for Shulamith's lack of sexual interest is simply that she was tired and already in bed. In a recent survey by Christian Family Life, 10 percent of the women indicated their number one sexual problem was tiredness.[9] It is quite likely a much higher percentage would have listed tiredness had the question included the first, second, and third major problems.

There are times a wife will be exhausted because of sick children, etc., and will perhaps be unable to climax. But as one loving wife put it, "she can still glory in pleasing her husband." If you are too tired to make love, there is nothing at all wrong with occasionally saying, "Honey, I just don't think I can climax tonight, but I'd love to make you happy." Then take him in your arms, give yourself to him, and whisper in his ear that you love him and are thrilled you can give him pleasure.

Furthermore, he should not be made to feel selfish if he makes such a request. You are not being "used" when you respond in this way (unless he makes a regular habit of it). You are showing your self-giving love. Can't you just enjoy being in his arms? There is no rule that a wife must reach orgasm every time. The central issue in sexual love is *not* having an orgasm; rather it is sharing mutual love.

Obviously, this kind of response would be a normal response in a vital and healthy marriage. However, if there are complex communication barriers, this response could seem foreign.

The Problem of Late-Night Sex

Solomon's late-night approach leaves much to be desired. Likewise, the late-night approach of many twentieth century husbands could stand some variation. Consider the following situation.

Typical Elmer, the average American husband, comes home from work just about the same way he left that morning—sparkling conversation, amorous embrace and all. He enters, nods briefly to the kids, grunts to his wife, asks if there was anything in the mail and then lets his mind be stimulated by blankly staring at the six o'clock news.

"Shhhh," his wife says to the children, "don't make any noise. Daddy is trying to watch TV."

At exactly the right time, his wife tiptoes into the TV room and says, "Dear, dinner is ready." (Elmer gets very upset when his dinner isn't ready on time.) He shares the latest moves in the office games, and she describes the latest neighborhood gossip and the children's misbehaviors. Wow! Exciting evening! Elmer burps his way through dinner and then leaves his wife to clean up the kitchen, diaper the kids, do the laundry, vacuum the house, write letters to *his* parents, and she falls asleep totally exhausted about nine-thirty. In the meantime, Elmer dozes off in front of "Tuesday Night at the Movies."

Suddenly, about 1:00 A.M. the "Star-Spangled Banner" jolts Elmer awake. He turns off the TV set, runs for his trusty javelin, dons his Roman toga, puts on a crown of ivy leaves, crashes into the bedroom and shouts, "Let the games begin." Elmer wants "play-time" before he goes "nite-nite." And of course she's supposed to be aroused and excited. Being very considerate, Elmer may even give her sixty seconds before "favoring" her with his "let's get down to business" virility. Good old hard-working Elmer just can't understand why his wife isn't passionately responding to his every initiative!

And even if she submits to her 1:00 A.M. husband with his spur-of-the-moment big ideas, she isn't likely to throw herself into it with the greatest of ardor.[10] Elmer is typical of many men who never seem to give their wives any attention until they want sex late at night. They demonstrate absolutely no involvement in their wives' problems or in their lives except when they are physically aroused.

Page Williams cites a humorous conversation he had with a little boy. He had asked the little lad what his dad did for a living, and the boy replied, "He watches."

Williams asked, "You mean he is a night watchman?"

"Oh, no," the little boy exclaimed, "He just watches."

"Well, what does he watch?" Williams asked.

"I don't know if I can tell you everything," he continued. "I can name a few things."

"Well, tell me," Williams replied.

"He watches TV, he watches Mom do the housework, he watches for the paperboy, he watches the weather, and I think he watches girls, too," he said, with an impish grin on his face. "He watches the stock market, football games, all the sports, he watches mother spank us, and he watches us do our homework. He watches us leave to go to church and PTA and shopping. He watches my brother mow the lawn, and he watches me rake. He watches my sister clean up the dirty dishes, and he watches me play with my dog. He watches Mom pay the bills. He watches *me* a lot—but mainly he just watches," said the little fellow, with a note of sadness in his voice.[11]

If you are a "typical Elmer" or a "watcher" don't expect much of a response sexually from your wife.

Solomon may not have been a "watcher," but he definitely needed some instruction on some appropriate times to approach his wife. I don't know if anyone has made a study of it, but my guess is that 90 percent or more of the times most couples make love are late at night after everything is done. They've eaten a full meal, cleaned up the kitchen, read the newspaper, helped the children with homework, discussed the family budget and stared blankly at the tube for three hours. Then they fall into bed for five or ten minutes of "ho-hum" sex followed immediately by snoring. After several years of this, sex "is just not that important to us." The vitality and spark of their sexual love is lost.

A gynecologist in Houston counsels young brides, "Never under any circumstances make love to your husband after 7:00 at night." This is an exaggeration, but Solomon could have profited from this information.

A late-night routine can kill sexual love. While many lovemaking experiences can "just happen," some of the most meaningful often are pre-planned. A phone call to your wife letting her know you love her and would like to set the evening aside for making love will go a long way toward getting her in the mood. A lingering good-bye kiss in the morning lets her know how much you'd rather stay home with her than go to work, and goes miles toward setting up an interesting evening.

While it's true Solomon was inconsiderate in his approach, her reaction is inspiring. Instead of sitting around feeling resentful, accusing him of wanting to "use her," and turning off sexually, she begins to work on her

A DREAM OF LOVE REFUSED

attitudes and *actions*. In Song 5:9-6:3 we see a decisive change of attitude, and in Song 7:1-13 we see a decisive change of action.

FOOTNOTES

1. Otto Zockler, *The Song of Songs (Lange's Commentary*, 12 Vols; Grand Rapids; Zondervan, 1960), V. 103.
2. *Ibid.*, V, 103.
3. S. Craig Glickman, *A Song for Lovers* (Downers Grove: Inter-Varsity, 1976), p. 63.
4. *Dallas Times Herald*, Nov. 12, 1973, p. 6-B.
5. Herbert Miles, *Sexual Happiness in Marriage* (Grand Rapids: Zondervan, 1967), p. 137.
6. Professor N. Junke, *Sex and Love Today* (New York: Vala, 1970), p. 125.
7. Miles, p. 137.
8. Shirley Rice, *Physical Unity in Marriage* (Norfolk: Tabernacle Church of Norfolk, 7120 Granby St., Norfolk, Va. 23505, 1973), p. 7-8.
9. Survey compiled by Christian Family Life, 9210 Markville, Dallas, Texas, 75231.
10. This illustration was adapted from a book by Lois Bird, Doubleday, Inc. Pub.
11. H. Page Williams, *Do Yourself A Favor, Love Your Wife* (Plainfield: Logos International, 1973), p. 5.

CHAPTER EIGHT
SOLVING SEXUAL PROBLEMS

(Reflections #10, 11, 12, Song 5:9–6:13)

In the last chapter we found Shulamith and Solomon involved in a frustrating problem in their physical relationship. In this section we see how they begin to solve their problems, and in Chapters 10 and 11 the ultimate solution unfolds.

Interestingly, the solution to their differences involved assuming personal responsibility for the error rather than focusing on the other's error. Instead of dwelling on how thoughtless Solomon was to continually approach her late at night, she began to work on her inner attitudes. Instead of thinking how selfish Shulamith is in rejecting him, Solomon concentrates on loving her unconditionally and "giving blessing for insult."

In order for any problem to be resolved in marriage, both partners must follow this pattern. What good is accomplished when you continually resent your mate for his or her shortcomings? When you and I stand before the judgment seat of Christ, He is not going to ask how our mate treated us, but whether or not we were faithful in assuming responsibility for our behavior. It is God's responsibility to deal with an offending mate, not ours.

A CHANGE OF ATTITUDE
(Reflection #10, Song 5:9-6:3)

CONTEXT

Shulamith has awakened from her dream-filled sleep the following morning. Before awakening, Shulamith asks the chorus to help her find her beloved. She wants him because she is highly aroused sexually (5:8), feels guilty about another rejection of Solomon (5:6,7), and wants to make amends. This address to the chorus provides a transition into the next scene. It gives the pretext for the chorus to ask two questions revealing Shulamith's decision to work on her attitude.

The first question is found in 5:9: "What kind of beloved is your beloved . . .?" The second is in 6:1: "Where has your beloved gone . . .?"

The answer to the first question calls Shulamith back to the nobility of her man and his physical attractiveness and tenderness. Thus, she begins to focus her thoughts on his positive traits and even his sexual appeal in order to increase her own desire.

The answer to the second question, "Where has your beloved gone . . .?" leads her to realize that much of their problem is due to the nature of the job he has, "pasturing the flock" (6:2)—tending the sheep (the people of Israel). As she thinks on this, she renews her covenant and finds assurance that he is totally hers even though some things need to be resolved (6:3).

COMMENTARY

5:9 CHORUS: What kind of beloved is your beloved,
O most beautiful among women?
What kind of beloved is your beloved,
Thus you adjure us?

SOLOMON ON SEX

What is the purpose of this question? It seems to be specifically designed by the chorus to lead Shulamith to focus on her husband's many good points. While there is pain at constant separation, they want her to realize it is worth it all in view of the excellent qualities of the man God has given her. The question has the intended effect; in the following verses she extols her beloved's virtues and expresses a relaxed acceptance of the fact he is away on the business of state (6:2-3).

5:10 SHULAMITH: My beloved is dazzling and ruddy,

The description that follows has some rather sensuous details that suggest she is reflecting on a previous lovemaking episode with him and pictures him nude in her mind. Again, it must be realized the daughters of Jerusalem are simply a literary device used, in this case, to bring out the excellences of the king.

To be "dazzling" is to be handsome, and to be "ruddy" means to have healthy, reddish cheeks.

Outstanding among ten thousand.

This is an expression of surpassing beauty.

5:11 SHULAMITH: His head is like gold, pure gold;

Beginning now with his head, she describes in matchless imagery his shapely body. Gold connotes excellence.

His locks are like clusters of dates,
And black as a raven.

Solomon has beautiful black hair. Ravens are known for their consistent ability to provide for their young. They are often used in terms of God's providential care of His creation.[1] She sees Solomon as always watching out for her.

5:12 SHULAMITH: His eyes are like doves,
Beside streams of water,
Bathed in milk,
And reposed in their setting.

The dark iris surrounded by the gleaming white of the eye is pictured as a dove bathing in milk.

5:13 SHULAMITH: His cheeks are like a bed of balsam,
Banks of sweet-scented herbs;

The bed of balsam refers to the custom of perfuming the beard.

His lips are lilies,
Dripping with liquid myrrh.

The lilies here are probably red lilies. The liquid myrrh probably refers to the sweetness of his breath. Often sweet, scented herbs were chewed to scent the breath or were mixed with water to make a mouthwash.

5:14 SHULAMITH: His hands are rods of gold

His fingers are full and round.

Set with beryl;

His fingernails are transparently pink.

His abdomen is carved ivory
Inlaid with sapphires.

The abdomen refers to the covered part of the body. It is white and smooth like ivory. To be like ivory means to be flat and firm. Also to see the "white" part of the body is to view that part which is normally shielded from the sun by clothing. It appears she is daydreaming about her husband's naked body. The reference to blue sapphires is difficult. It probably refers to the branching blue veins under the white skin.[2]

5:15 SHULAMITH: His legs are pillars of alabaster
set on pedestals of gold;

The phrase "legs" is often used of the upper part of the legs. It denotes the loins (Gen. 29:2; Exod. 28:42; Dan. 2:32) or the part of the body where the legs begin to separate.[3] They are alabaster, strong and white like marble. They are set on feet described as pedestals of gold.

His appearance is like Lebanon,
Choice as the cedars.

SOLOMON ON SEX

Lebanon speaks of majestic appearances. It was famed for its fertility and beauty (Deut. 3:25). The cedars were the tallest and strongest of trees; so is her beloved outstanding among men. It speaks of his strength and masculinity.

> 5:16 SHULAMITH: His mouth is full of sweetness.
> And he is wholly desirable.
> This is my beloved and this is my friend,
> O daughters of Jerusalem.

This refers to the mouth as an organ of speech, not of kissing. She is praising his tender speech. The thing that appealed to her wasn't just his physical manliness (5:9-15), but his tenderness and gentleness with her (5:16). Paul says God's "lover" has these two characteristics.

> For the husband is the head of the wife as Christ is the head of the church (Eph. 5:23).

A man is supposed to be a "head," a leader, to his wife. But at the same time Paul says,

> Husbands, love your wives, just as Christ loved the church (Eph. 5:25).

He is also to be a *lover*. It was said of the Lord Jesus,

> The Word became flesh and lived for a while among us. We have seen His glory, the glory of the One and only Son, who came from the Father, full of *grace* and *truth* (John 1:14).

The husband, then, is to be characterized by strength and tenderness (Song 5:9–16); he is to be a leader and a lover (Eph. 5:23–25); and he is to be full of truth and grace (John 1:14). These are the basic characteristics of the male role as revealed in the Bible. The Lord Jesus was a man of grace; He cried in the presence of women, he made little children feel at home with Him, and He demonstrated profound tenderness and compassion. But He could also walk through an angry mob, refrain from accusing His accusers, set His will like steel, and be obedient unto death.

Many problems in marriages today go back to husbands who have one of these characteristics out of balance.

6:1 CHORUS: Where has your beloved gone,
O most beautiful among women?
Where has your beloved turned,
That we may seek him with you?

The chorus is satisfied with the answer, and now a new question is in their mouths. Its purpose is to focus Shulamith's attention on the fact that the reason he cannot be with her now is that he is involved in affairs of state. She is, therefore, to remember the understanding she had before they were married and to choose to reject the thought of self-pity she feels at not having Solomon at her side as much as she would like.

6:2 SHULAMITH: My beloved has gone down to his garden,
To the beds of balsam,
To pasture his flock in the gardens
And gather lilies.

As discussed elsewhere (1:7; 2:16) this imagery refers to Solomon's preoccupation with the affairs of state.

6:3 SHULAMITH: I am my beloved's and my beloved is mine,
He who pastures his flock among the lilies.

Shulamith has come to inner peace. She is a king's wife. He must be away on business, but she confidently asserts her belief in his love for her.

It is significant that Shulamith views her husband as a shepherd who pastures his flock. Despite all of Solomon's shortcomings, he makes her feel totally loved, protected, and cared for. She sees him not only as Israel's shepherd, but as her shepherd.

There are two outstanding characteristics of a shepherd that are applicable here. He was a *protector* and *leader*. Much can be said about the protective qualities of the shepherd.[4]* His main task, other than providing for his flock, was protecting them from robbers, animals, and weather.

The shepherd's staff, a stick five or six feet long which sometimes had a crook at the end, was used in the way Western men use a cane or walking stick. It is also used in handling the sheep. Thus, when David writes in Psalm 23, "Thy rod and Thy staff, they comfort me," he is saying the Lord's protection comforts him, and he feels safe.

*All the following material on the protective qualities of the shepherd are taken from Fred Wright's *Manners and Customs of Bible Lands* (Moody, 1953).

SOLOMON ON SEX

Elements of protection embrace sacrificial labors of love. The fact that the shepherd dedicated his life to his flock, even to the point of losing his life, demonstrates emphatically his care and concern for them. (Granted, he had a vested interest, but don't husbands have a vested interest in pleasing their wives?) A good husband must also be willing to "lay down his life DAILY" for his wife. Laying down one's life daily in most cases is more difficult than a once and for all physical death. "Husbands, love your wives, just as Christ also loved the church *and gave Himself up for her*" (Eph. 5:25).

Why? Because like begets like. When you say, "I willingly sacrifice my wants for your wants," this produces a like response in her. Perhaps at first this new task will evoke amazement, curiosity, or a "how-long-will-this-last" attitude, but eventually it evokes appreciation, thankfulness, and "I willingly sacrifice my wants for your wants" too. Love begets love; encouragement begets encouragement; concern, concern.

As a leader, the Eastern shepherd never drives his sheep as does the Western shepherd. He *leads them*, usually going before them. He may also walk by their sides and sometimes follow behind, especially if the flock is headed for the fold in the evening. From the rear he can gather any stragglers and protect them from wild animal attacks.

Several flocks are sometimes allowed to mix at a well or in the same fold. When it becomes necessary to separate the flocks, one shepherd after another calls out his own call. The sheep lift their heads and, after a general scramble, begin following each one after his own shepherd. They are thoroughly familiar with their own shepherd's *tone of voice*. Strangers have often used the same call, but their attempts to get the sheep to follow them always fail.

Jesus implied His sheep hear and follow only His voice when He said, "The sheep follow Him, for they know His voice. And a stranger will they not follow, but will flee from him: for they know not the voice of strangers" (John 10:4,5). The intimate concern and care of the shepherd is the key reason the sheep follow *only his voice*. They *know him* and thus they TRUST his leading (especially when he has proven trustworthy in the past).

To illustrate the intimate knowledge and concern a good shepherd has for his sheep, we cite the following example.

One shepherd in the Lebanon district was asked if he always counted his sheep each evening. He replied in the negative, and then was asked how then he knew if all his sheep were present. This was his reply: "Master, if you were to put a cloth over my eyes, and bring me any sheep and only let me put hands on its face, I could tell in a moment if it was mine or not.

When H. R. P. Dickson visited the desert Arabs, he witnessed an event that revealed the amazing knowledge some of them have of their sheep.

One evening, shortly after dark, an Arab shepherd began to call out one by one the names of his fifty-one mother sheep, and was able to pick out each one's lamb and restore it to its mother to suckle. To do this in the light would be a feat for many shepherds, but this was done in complete darkness, and in the midst of the noise of the ewes crying for their lambs, and the lambs crying for their mothers.

But no oriental shepherd ever had a more intimate knowledge of his sheep than Jesus our great Shepherd has of those who belong to His flock. He once said of Himself: "I am the good shepherd, and know my sheep" (John 10:14).

Most women want to be led. They do not want to be browbeaten, treated as imbeciles unable to think or decide, or coddled as children too immature to make decisions. That is not leadership, but dictatorship, and does not take into consideration the needs of the followers, but only the haughty ego of the "leader."

Thus, Shulamith's "daydreaming" reveals two fundamental attitudes helpful for the resolution of their sexual differences. She first thinks of her husband physically as a means of increasing her desire for him. She then thinks of the protective care and security he has provided as her shepherd. So instead of concentrating on his weaknesses, she concentrates on his strengths. She assumes responsibility for her personal attitudes and leaves Solomon's shortcomings in the Lord's hands.

THE RETURN OF SOLOMON
(Reflection #11, Song 6:4-10)

In the interlude between their problem (5:2-8) and its solution (7:1-8:13), two fundamental attitudes are revealed. In the preceeding reflection we see Shulamith concentrating on his strengths. Now, in this reflection the poet directs us to another crucial ingredient in resolving marital tension; we must learn to respond to insult with a blessing.

As this scene opens, Solomon has returned. He praises her beauty and gives her assurance of his exclusive love for her. Consistently throughout the Song, Solomon is an excellent example. Whatever tensions may have developed in their relationship (5:4-6), they do not appear to affect Solomon's expressions of love and praise for her.

Most husbands, when rebuffed after making a sexual overture to their wives, tend to withdraw into a shell or react in a "cutting" way. But Solomon demonstrates true love, always responds properly, and lovingly demonstrates much patience and confidence in the Lord to work things out.

6:4 SOLOMON: You are as beautiful as Tirzah, my darling,
As lovely as Jerusalem,

Tirzah was an old Canaanite city famous for its beauty and renowned as the royal residence of kings after Solomon died. Shulamith is from a higher mountainous region of the North, and Tirzah is located in the mountains of the North also.[5]

As awesome as an army with banners.

Why is Shulamith as awesome as an army in full battle array? Because she has exerted upon Solomon a fearful power with her beautiful eyes that pierce his heart and vanquish all resistance.

6:5 SOLOMON: Turn your eyes away from me,
For they have confused me;

One penetrating glance from her eyes causes Solomon's heart to melt. Solomon then launches into a repeat of her beauties expressed on the wedding night (4:1–7).

Your hair is like a flock of goats
That have descended from Gilead (see 4:1).

6:6 SOLOMON: Your teeth are a flock of ewes
Which have come up from their washing,
All of which bear twins,
And not one among them has lost her young (see 4:2).

6:7 SOLOMON: Your temples are like a slice of a pomegranate
Behind your veil (see 4:3).

Note the fact that the praise Solomon gives her here is almost exactly identical to that which he bestowed upon her on their wedding night

119

(4:1–3). In effect, Solomon seems to say, "Nothing has changed. Regardless of how you respond toward me, this does not affect the love I have for you. I still view you as I always have, even though in some points your performance has not been up to the standards that I would desire."

To adopt this kind of attitude shows Solomon truly loves her as Christ loves the church (Eph. 5:25). Christ loves us consistently regardless of how we perform. That does not mean the Shulamite should not improve her performance if it needs improving, just as we need to improve our performance in our relationship to Christ. But she should not be under a law to perform in order to gain acceptance. Consider 1 Pet. 3:7 in this connection:

You husbands likewise, live with your wives in an understanding way . . .

The verb translated "live with" is consistently translated in the Septuagint translation of the Old Testament as "have sexual intercourse with" (Deut. 22:13; 24:1; 21:13; 22:22; 25:5; Isa. 62:5; Gen. 20:3). The phrase "an understanding way" implies acquiring knowledge and insight through a process of personal investigation. Thus an interpretive and expanded paraphrase of the verse might read:

You husbands likewise, have sexual intercourse with your wife in a way that is based upon insight gathered from personal investigation of her needs.

Then in this connection consider 1 Pet. 3:9:

Not returning evil for evil, or insult for insult, but giving a blessing instead; for you were called for the very purpose that you might inherit a blessing.

Part of having a sexual relationship with your mate in an understanding way is *not* to respond with insult when hurt, but to respond with blessing—with love and appreciation for his or her strong qualities. Solomon's ego was undoubtedly severely slapped when she refused his love, but he reciprocated by praising her and seeking her best instead of responding to insult.

Many husbands are concerned with how to get their wives to be more sexual and aggressive. A sure way to hinder them is to respond with insult when they do not perform the way they are supposed to. This simply drives a wedge into the relationship, ultimately leading to complete loss of interest on the wife's part and causing greater sexual problems.

SOLOMON ON SEX

Note the promise in 3:10 to the husband and wife if they respond properly:

For let him who means to *love life* and see *good days* refrain his tongue from evil . . .

If you want things to improve in your relationship, be sure your response to any offense your mate gives in sexual matters is honoring to the Lord.

Solomon continues his praise,

6:8 SOLOMON: There are sixty queens and eighty concubines,
        And maidens without number;

6:9 SOLOMON: But my dove, my perfect one, is unique:

We have already discussed the matter of Solomon's polygamy (Chapter 1). He may not have been a practicing polygamist at this time. We know he inherited a harem from his father, David. The passing on of the harem from king to successor has long been observed. Roland de Vaux observes, "It appears that the king's harem, at least in the early days of the monarchy, used to pass to his successor."[6]

Thus Solomon may not have been sexually involved with these many concubines until later in his reign, when we know he began to degenerate into lustful polygamy. But whether or not he was does not detract from the validity of the principles he teaches. Furthermore, God has put His approval on the principles by making the Song of Solomon a part of Scripture.

But what is the point of the comparison? He says she is superior to all the queens and concubines in the empire. The concubine in the ancient Near East had two basic functions. A barren wife might have sons through her.[7] But secondly, they were for a man's "delight." Solomon comments on this in Eccles. 2:8 where he says,

I heaped up for myself also silver and gold, and the peculiar property of kings and of countries; I got men singers and women singers; and the *delights* of the children of men: *mistress* and *mistresses*.[8]

The Hebrew word translated "delights" here refers to sexual caresses and enjoyments of the pleasures of sexual love.[9] It is the same word used of Shulamith in Song 7:6, "How beautiful and *delightful* you are"—skilled in giving sexually delightful caresses. Thus, a concubine was a kind of mistress.

The twentieth century call girl would to some extent parallel the concubine, except these modern-day "mistresses" have abandoned the child-bearing aspect! They simply provide skilled sexual pleasure. The business world is full of these immoral young women. While the skills they supposedly have are common knowledge, only a husband not satisfied at home or deprived sexually by his wife would tend to be interested. If a man doesn't have a "magnet" at home, he might look elsewhere! This is what Paul warns against.

> Stop depriving one another, except by agreement for a time that you may devote yourselves to prayer, and come together again lest *Satan tempt you because of your lack of self-control.* (1 Cor. 7:5)

He implies if a husband and wife do not satisfy each other sexually, both or one might be tempted by Satan to get that satisfaction somewhere else! The best prevention for adultery is complete satisfaction at home.

> 6:8 SOLOMON: There are sixty queens and eighty concubines,
> And maidens without number;
> But my dove, my perfect one, is unique:

He is saying Shulamith is superior in every way to any concubine of the empire. Even though Solomon may not have been sexually involved with any of these women at that time, he knows about their "skills" just as we hear today. Shulamith is superior as a lovemaking partner. She is more "skilled" than any of them!

I'll never forget the message my wife heard by one of the most godly Christian women I ever met. Her testimony has been written in a number of books. She is the wife of one of the most prominent evangelical leaders of our time and is a widely sought-after speaker to women's groups all over the country. She was speaking to a group of wives on the subject of sex in marriage.

In essence she said the following: "You know, girls, a prostitute is skilled in all the techniques of giving sexual pleasure to a man she does not even know or love. If they can do that for a man they do not even know or love, just for money, surely we should be even more skilled in giving sexual pleasure to our husbands whom we do love."

Shulamith was superior to all would-be mistresses in her husband's eyes—are you? Solomon said this was true of Shulamith, and this book presents sex in marriage as the "flame of the Lord" (8:6).

The same idea is implied in Prov. 5:1-23.

An Immoral Harlot	A Loving Wife
"Keep your way far from her," 5:8	"Drink water from your own cistern" 5:15
	"Rejoice in the wife of your youth" 5:18
	"Be exhilarated always with her love" 5:19
	"Let her breasts satisfy you at all times" 5:19
5:1 5:14	5:15 5:23

Wives, are your husbands rejoicing in, being exhilarated by, and being satisfied with your skill in making love? The contrast of the temptation of a harlot with the love of a wife certainly suggests a wife ought to have more to offer her man physically than a professional mistress!

I would like to conclude this discussion by posing a question for you wives to ask yourselves. Please do not think I am advocating immorality when I ask you to ask it. But, if your husband began to search out a mistress, would he select you? Would you qualify—sexually, I mean? If not, then you might consider a few changes.

Solomon has praised his wife above all the women in his court. In the following verses he deals with some of the reasons he praises her.

6:9 SOLOMON: But my dove, my perfect one, is unique:
                 She is her mother's only daughter;
                 She is the pure child of the one who bore her.

The phrase suggests she was her mother's favorite.

         The maidens saw her and called her blessed
         The queens and concubines also, they
            praised her, saying

6:10 SOLOMON: Who is this that grows like the dawn,

"She outshines all others like the early dawn, which looks down from heaven over the mountains down to the earth," Zockler says.[10]

> As beautiful as a full moon,
> As pure as the sun,

She had blazing radiance. Arabic poets frequently compared feminine beauty to the sun and the moon.

> As awesome as an army with banner. (See 6:4)

SHULAMITH IN THE GARDEN
(Reflection #12, Song 6:11-13a)

In this section Shulamith takes her leave of Solomon and goes to a garden on the palace grounds for meditation. Previously she had two problems: (1) guilt at refusing Solomon's advances and (2) a desire to see the countryside once again. Solomon's lavish praise assuring his acceptance of her just as she is has dealt with the first problem. Only one remains—a desire to return to the country she left.

The logical connection of this scene to the preceding verses seems to be it is the answer to the question raised in 6:10 ("Who is this that grows like the dawn?"). Shulamith's answer, as the scene will reveal, is that she is a country girl in the palace of a king, one whose soul is craving to visit the Lebanon mountains she loves.

The scene involves a dialogue with the imaginary chorus.

> 6:11 SHULAMITH: I went down to the orchard of nut trees
> To see the blossoms of the valley,

The passage suggests the springtime once again. Perhaps her thoughts went back to Solomon's springtime visit during their courtship.

> To see whether the vine had budded
> Or the pomegranates had bloomed.
>
> Before I was aware, my soul set me
> Over the chariots of my noble people.

This is the most difficult verse in the book to interpret. Although

SOLOMON ON SEX

interpretations differ tremendously, it seems that we must take verse 13 into account, ("Come back, come back, O Shulammite"), implies Shulamith is entertaining the thought of leaving the palace.

The thought seems to be this: Shulamith is in the garden quietly meditating on the beauty around her and thinking of home. Gradually her thoughts begin to drift back to life in the palace. She thinks of the lonesome hours she spends waiting for Solomon's attention and often feels alone and forsaken, a country girl in a king's palace.

As she is absorbed in her thoughts, the sound of a chariot bounding along a distant road breaks the hush of the morning. Suddenly the desire comes upon her to get in one of the chariots and flee the palace. The text makes it quite clear that she does not do so, but her "soul set her over (in) the chariots"—her heart longed to be in one. She is not thinking of forsaking Solomon; rather it is a sudden impulse to flee to the country she loved. The chariots of her noble people refer to the chariots which belong to the retinue of the court.

6:13 CHORUS: Come back, come back, O Shulamite

The chorus calls her longing heart back to reality by saying "Come back," psychologically speaking, four times. This is the first time the word *Shulammite* is used in the book. Without doubt the word is the feminine form of "Solomon."[11] It suggests she is the "other part of" Solomon. She is one flesh with him. That realization brings her thoughts back to her lover and her desire to make love with him.

Come back that we may gaze at you!

COMMENT

Of shepherds and sex

A shepherd is a *protector* and a *leader*. As a husband, are you? If you are not and you find your wife is not particularly responsive sexually, it could be related to these factors. The number one concern of men, according to one survey, in their sexual relationship with their wives, is that their wives are not aggressive enough. This survey indicates that 19 percent of Christian husbands (that's one out of every five men who read this book) complain of their wife's lack of interest in sex.[12] Have you considered the relationship between your leadership and her loving? Let me explain.

God has obviously set up a line of authority in all spheres of human existence (family, church, government). He has done so for good reason. No one can carry all the responsibility. Thus, the person over you in your job does not require you to shoulder his responsibilities as well as yours. Yet, too many wives are bearing responsibilities God never intended them to carry. For example, in your family, who carries the *emotional* burden for how your children turn out? Who carries the emotional burden for their discipline? According to the Bible, she is not to carry that burden; you and I are! (Eph. 6:1-4)

The thing that makes the chain of command work is its capacity to absorb shock. Something is always going wrong in life. Does that something always crash in on your wife, or is it intercepted and absorbed by you?

This works in the business world. A firm on the West Coast recently received a number of awards for outstanding business achievement. Yet, in their everyday workings, they violated many basic principles of sound business management. An examination into the inner working revealed that the reason for this firm's success was three men. These men were shock absorbers. Every time financial collapse, business reversal, personal problem, or legal hassle threatened the firm, these men absorbed the shock. As the shock waves began to wind their way down the chain of command, they ran smash into these three men and stopped!

As a result, the employees underneath them came to work free from worry and pressure. They didn't have to absorb the pressures of their supervisors and they therefore produced to their maximum.

Your wife is like one of those employees. When the shock waves of life's reversal come crashing in on your family, if there is a man there to absorb them and to provide a protective shield, she is emotionally released to be a woman. I'm not saying you shouldn't ever share your problems with her. You should share them all with her. She is a joint heir of the grace of life. One of the reasons you married her was because she was a source of strength. The issue is, how do you share your problems?

Do you do it in a depressing, defeated, and complaining way that simply burdens her with not only her sphere of problems but now yours too? Or do you do it like this, "Honey, we've really got some things we need to trust the Lord for. I've been laid off, and there are no job prospects and no money. Right now I have no idea what we are going to do, but I know that God has a purpose in it, and I'm really looking forward to what He is going to do. Let's pray and trust this situation to Him."

Thus, instead of dumping the problem on her and asking her to prop

SOLOMON ON SEX

you up, you've asked her to join you in trusting the problem to the Lord. What makes the difference is your attitude. We're not saying you have to be the strong silent type that smiles as he leads his troops into battle with both legs shot off, but if you are continually whining and communicating weakness to her, she can't be expected to follow your lead with much confidence in bed or anywhere else.

If you are a protector and a leader, if you assume personal responsibility for that home and for her welfare and happiness, if you assume responsibility for the kids, the bills, the family's future, its goals, you are a shepherd like Solomon. Furthermore, you are creating an atmosphere in which she feels secure and trusting. You are creating a climate that makes her feel she can trust in you and rely on you.

How is being a shepherd related to sexual love?

In a massive study of 500 women covering five years, Seymour Fisher came to some startling conclusions about one of the most common sexual problems among women—inability to experience orgasm. Some studies have indicated that as many as 40 percent of American women married twenty years or more have never experienced orgasm. In a study I conducted of some 158 women, 39 percent indicated they experienced orgasm "sometimes, rarely, or never."[13]

One of the common characteristics of a large percentage of non-orgasmic wives in Fisher's study was feelings about loss. "Overall, there was enough evidence to suggest that a woman's ability to reach orgasm is tied to her feelings about loss. Apparently, the more she feels that she cannot depend on being able to hold onto the people and things she values, the more limited is her orgasm capacity."[14]

Thus, if there is an insecure atmosphere about your relationship, there will be a sense of loss. If she doesn't feel totally secure, she will be afraid to "let go." If she feels your relationship is tenuous, that you are unstable and unpredictable, her inner security is disrupted.

Recently I heard a good illustration. A man up on the roof is trying to fix his TV antenna. Suddenly it begins to rain, and as he struggles with the guy wires, he slips. He begins to tumble down the roof, makes a last ditch effort and grabs the drain trough. He is hanging from the edge some three stories up, and his fingers begin to give way. Desperately he struggles to hold on, but his strength is almost gone. Not knowing what else to do, he looks up into the sky and asks, "Is there anyone up there who can help me?"

Sure enough, a little cloud forms and parts in two, and a voice booms out from behind the cloud, "Believe and let go."

The man hangs there staring blankly into the heaven for about thirty seconds and then shouts, "Is there anyone *else* up there who can help me?"

Before that man will "believe and let go," he wants to know the voice can back up its command. He wants to know someone will be there to catch him before he hits the ground. He wants a sense of trust and confidence in the "somebody."

The same situation applies to a wife as she moves toward orgasm. Men and women tend to conceptualize sexual intercourse in slightly different ways. A man tends to think of intercourse as a taking or a possessing. A woman, on the other hand, tends to see it as a yielding, a giving of herself. Thus for her to be totally free, she must feel secure in the permanence of your love and the security of your relationship with her.

As she is moving toward orgasm, the sexual tension develops gradually to a point where there is a blurring of perceptual reality. As objects become hazy she may picture the relationship "slipping away." To yield totally is like "Believe, and let go." Perception is fading and she now must "let go." Yield. If there is any insecurity or lack of trust in the marriage relationship, she may subconsciously pull back and cannot "let go" as perceptual reality darkens. She transfers her lack of security and permanance in the relationship outside the bedroom into the bed itself, and it sets up a mental block that keeps her from moving to a climax.

This is by no means the only reason women do not achieve orgasms, but it appears to be a major one. I know many men who are wonderful "shepherds" whose wives have never experienced an orgasm; however, all too frequently the problem is rooted in a lack of a trusting and secure relationship.

She wants to feel you are a man . . . that you will protect her, lead her, and take care of her forever. If you communicate indifference, weakness, or deliberate insensitivity, you can upset the balance of her emotional mechanism. Thus, sexual problems are usually relationship problems and not just the woman's problem.

"Why don't you go see a doctor and find out what's wrong with you?" some husbands ask. There is nothing wrong with her in most cases; there is something wrong with your relationship, and that is just as much your fault as hers.

One well-known sexual treatment clinic has come to a dogmatic conclusion that there is no such thing as a woman with the problem of "frigidity." There are only marriage relationships with the problem of frigidity. The relationship is the problem, not the woman!

SOLOMON ON SEX

Edgar Rice Bourroughs had the right idea about male-female relationships when he told the Tarzan stories. An ape-man in the jungles of Africa was raised by some gorillas. One day a woman named Jane (Ph.D. in something), came into Tarzan's world, and he married her. Tarzan knew what he wanted, and Jane knew what she wanted—Tarzan. She may have had a Ph.D., but Tarzan called the shots. Once they got that straightened out, they had a swinging time together! He offered security, strength, and protection!

A love affair with your husband's body

Shulamith has a love affair with her husband's body. She daydreams erotically of his physical manliness. She has a problem getting her sexual desire up to Solomon's, so one way she raises it is to think sexual thoughts about her husband during the day. Shirley Rice speaks of having a "holy lust" for your husband. Shulamith did (Song 5:9–16).

Do you think about your husband sexually or do you just think of "what a nice guy he is"? Do you think of how great it is to make love with him, or do you think of him as "that wonderful father and provider"? It is perfectly "holy" to think erotic, sexual thoughts about your husband during the day. It's in the Bible.

Too frequently women who cannot climax tend to view their husband's genitals as separate from their husband as a person. They would never daydream about their husband's body as Shulamith did; it seems repulsive to them. This is a major cause of orgasmic dysfunction. You are to consider his genitals as part of him as a person. You are to consider his semen as life, his life! This is easy to grasp in connection with conception and pregnancy, but not in regard to sex.

Three basic attitudes for solving problems

This series of three reflections reveals three basic attitudes adopted by Shulamith and Solomon in the interim between the beginning of the sexual problems and their solution. These attitudes are crucial for the resolution of all marital problems.

First there is the assuming of responsibility for one's own behavior instead of blaming the mate.

The second basic attitude necessary for problem-solving is to render a blessing when hurt or offended by one's mate (1 Pet. 3:9).

The third basic attitude revealed here is a complete and transparent communication of one's real feelings. To suggest marriage problems can be solved by simply assuming responsibility for one's own behavior and responding with a blessing is quite simplistic and can lead to suppression of negative feelings. It is vitally important that all negative feelings be freely and totally vented. Even anger should be fully expressed.

The Scriptures admonish us to "be angry but sin not" (Eph. 4:26). I think this means our anger is never to dissolve into personal attacks, bitterness, or name calling. An "explosion" of pent-up tensions in a marital relationship can often have a very healthy effect. If you have been hurt by your mate, by all means express your hurt and reveal your feelings. How else can he work on the problem unless he knows specifically what it is? On the other hand, continual nagging and criticism is counter-productive.

Make your feelings known and strive for as few "reminders" as possible, trusting God to work changes. If there seems to be no response, professional help should be considered before the communication lines become so frozen that it becomes impossible to find release in the relationship.

The two lovers of the Song are well on their way to resolving some of the problems they encountered in regard to sexual compatibility. The first step in the direction of a solution involved a change of attitude. Now, in the following reflection, a change of *action* is apparent as Shulamith aggressively takes the initiative in their loveplay.

FOOTNOTES

1. *The Interpreters Dictionary of the Bible*, ed. Arthur Buttrick, 4 Vols. (New York: Abingdon Press, 1962), 4, 13.
2. Franz Delitzsch, *Song of Songs* (Grand Rapids: Eerdmans, n.d.), p. 104.
3. Otto Zockler, *The Song of Solomon Lange's Commentary*, 12 Vols.; Grand Rapids: Zondervan, 1960 [orig. ed. 1872]), V. 107.
4. Fred Hartley Wright, *Manners and Customs of Bible Lands* (Moody, 1953).
5. Delitzsch, p. 109.
6. Roland de Vaux, *Ancient Israel* (New York: McGraw-Hill, 1965), p. 116.
7. *Interpreters Dictionary of the Bible*, I, 666.
8. Translation by Delitzsch, p. 238.
9. Zockler, *Ecclesiastes,* p. 56.
10. Zockler, *Song*, p. 111.
11. H. H. Rowley, "The Meaning of the 'Shulamite,'" *The American Journal of Semitic Languages and Literature*, 56 (January, 1939), 84-91.
12. Christian Family Life Marital Information Survey, 1974.
13. *Ibid.*
14. Seymour Fisher, *Understanding the Female Orgasm*, p. 74.

CHAPTER NINE
THE DANCE OF THE MAHANAIM

(Reflection #13, Song 6:13b–8:4)

CONTEXT

In the previous reflection, the Chorus has called Shulamith back, psychologically, to her home in the palace. They say:

> 6:13 CHORUS: Come back, come back, O Shulammite;
> Come back, come back, that we may gaze at you.

This serves as a transition to the next scene. The point of transition is in the word "gaze." The chorus, an imaginary literary device, obviously will not do the gazing on Shulamith. But the idea of "gazing" is picked up in the next scene as Solomon gazes on the beauties of his wife as she dances before him—(they are alone in the palace).

The logical connection with the preceding scenes seems to be this. Shulamith awakens after a painful dream only to find Solomon is not at her side. The dream has set her desires in motion to make love with her husband (5:8). Solomon appears and assures her of his love regardless of her performance (6:4–10). Then Solomon returns to the palace, and Shulamith goes down into the garden to be alone with her thoughts. Her longings for her country home are interrupted by the urgent plea of the chorus to come back, psychologically speaking, to life at the palace. Her thoughts are suddenly drawn once again to her lover, the desire she had to be in his arms (5:8) is rekindled, and she seeks him out in the following passage to make love. Solomon had approached her desiring to make love many times and at the wrong times, and she had refused him. Now she picks up on her intent of 5:6–8 to search out her husband and initiate lovemaking with him (6:13b–7:9).

Thus, even though much of the problem is Solomon's fault, she assumes responsibility for her own behavior. In 5:10–6:3 she changes her *attitude*, and in 6:13b–8:4 changes her *actions*.

COMMENTARY

Solomon and Shulamith are alone in the palace. Shulamith desires to make love with her husband and aggressively takes the initiative. As part of their loveplay, and as her way of arousing her husband's sexual interest, she dances before him. She obviously has no problems with inhibitions.

> 6:13b SHULAMITH (to the Chorus):
> Why should you gaze at the Shulammite
> As at the dance of two companies?

As Shulamith dances before her lover, she is being very coy and saying, "Why would the chorus want to gaze on me?" The answer is obvious; Solomon thinks she is beautiful and loves to look at her. She is replying to the quotation of the imaginary chorus of 6:13a. This statement provides a literary and logical transition from one point in the Song to another. The following verses clearly indicate this to be a very close, intimate scene involving Shulamith and Solomon and the conversation of love, *alone!* (7:6, 10)

What is the "dance of two companies?" The phrase "two companies" is a translation of the Hebrew word, "mahanaim." Mahanaim was a town from which David fled as a fugitive from Absolom (2 Sam. 17:24). It was a small town situated north of the Jabbok, not far from the Jordan Valley. The allusion here seems to be the appearance of the angelic host at this site to Jacob on his return home to the promised land. It is not clear why Solomon refers to Mahanaim. Perhaps, the dance of the Mahanaim contains something as magnificent and transporting as an angel's dance. Perhaps he viewed Shulamith as an "angel" dancing before him.

Dancing like this may seem strange to Western tastes, but in the East in the Old Testament conception, joy and dancing were inseparable (Eccles. 3:4)—joy not only as the happy feeling of youthful life, but also spiritual and holy joy (Ps. 87:7).

Zockler argues convincingly that the descriptive phrases to follow are from Solomon's lips.[1]

> 7:1 How beautiful are your feet in sandals
> O prince's daughter

Solomon comments on the gracefulness of her dancing.

> The curves of your hips are like jewels
> The work of the hands of an artist

Both Lehrman and Delitzsch agree the curves of the hips refer to their swaying motion as she dances before Solomon.[2] The phrase "curves of hips" is translated by Delitzsch, "the vibration of thy thighs."[3] These movements are of a circular motion, and probably refer to the windings of the upper part of the body by means of the thigh joint.

Thus, Shulamith is dancing before her husband as part of their love-play. The reference to the top part of her thighs, her navel, her belly, and her breasts indicates she had little or no clothing on.

> 7:2a Your navel is like a round goblet
> which never lacks mixed wine

The word "navel" is assuredly an incorrect translation, probably reflecting the translator's modesty. While the Hebrew word could take that meaning, it is generally translated today as "vulva," according to Brown, Driver, & Briggs.[4] In other words, Solomon views his wife's "garden" as she dances nude before him, and she/him, and he says it looks to him like a "round goblet." The *Hebrew* for "round goblet"

133

should be rendered "a bowl in the shape of a half moon."[5] The allusion to the female genitals is obvious; furthermore, this interpretation is necessary in view of the sequential progression upward of his description of his wife, similar to the sequence in 4:1–8.

(10) hair—tresses 7:5
(9) head—crowns you like carmel 7:5
(8) nose—like a tower of Lebanon 7:4
(7) eyes—pools in Heshbon 7:4
(6) neck—tower of ivory 7:4
(5) breasts—two fawns 7:3
(4) belly—heap of wheat 7:2
(3) "garden"—navel—bowl in shape of a half moon 7:2
(2) upper part of thighs—roundings of hips 7:2
(1) feet—7:1

For "navel" to mean "belly button" would violate the obvious sequence of the passage.

Solomon says his wife's garden never lacks mixed wine. Wine is used throughout the book (see 1:2, 2:4, 5:1) and in Eastern erotic poems as a symbol of sexual pleasure. It would appear that Solomon is suggesting that her "garden" is a never-lacking source of sexual pleasure for him. It is probable that the "mixed wine" refers to a mixing of his sexual pleasure with hers—of wine and milk (5:1); of myrrh and balsam.

7:2b SOLOMON: Your belly is like a heap of wheat
Fenced about with lilies.

In Syria, the perfect skin was considered to be that which could be compared in color to the yellowish-white of wheat after it had been threshed and winnowed.[6] Her navel and stomach are described as being composed of wine and wheat. These symbols suggest the common associations of a meal. Thus, the joining of these two images implies that her "navel" and stomach constitute a feast.[7] It indicates a desire to kiss these areas as he later expresses a desire to kiss her breasts.

7:3 SOLOMON: Your two breasts are like two fawn,
Twins of a gazelle (see 4:5).
Your neck is like a tower of ivory

Her neck is smooth, white, and long.

SOLOMON ON SEX

> Your eyes like the pools of Heshbon.

This was a city noted for its soft and beautiful pools. The symbolism indicates peace in her eyes.

> By the gate of Bath-rabbim.

The gates of a city were the chief places of assembly.

> Your nose is like the tower of Lebanon
> Which faces toward Damascus.

A tower facing Damascus was for the protection of the nation. "In a like manner her stately look perhaps reflected the strong character which was her protection, says one author.[8]

7:5 SOLOMON: Your head crowns you like Carmel
And the flowing locks of your head
are like purple threads,
The king is captivated by your tresses.

As majestic Mt. Carmel crowned the fertile plains of Palestine, so her beautiful face sits exquisitely atop her lovely figure. Since purple was the royal color, he must see her hair as "queenly." While chains could not hold this mighty king, Shulamith's lovely tresses have bound him to her.

7:6 SOLOMON: How beautiful and delightful you are,
My love, with all your charms.
7:7   Your stature is like a palm tree
And your breasts are like its clusters.

She has a stately stature. To look upon the clusters of the date palm causes the beholder to want to taste them. This simile of subjective response, then, suggests Solomon's desire to kiss her breasts.

The palm tree serves as a very beautiful description of Solomon's beloved. It sways in the wind with inexpressible gracefulness but seldom breaks. The trunk was tall, slender, and flexible.[9] Palm branches were traditionally a source of rejoicing (Lev. 23:4; Neh. 8:15; Rev. 7:9).[10] The tree typified grace, elegance, and uprightness.[11]

7:8 SOLOMON: I said "I will climb the palm tree
I will take hold of its fruit stalks."
Oh may your breasts be like clusters
of the vine.

To "climb the palm tree" had a special meaning. In the Ancient Near East the artificial fertilization of the female palm tree flowers by the male palm tree flowers has been practiced from earliest times. The male and female flowers are born on separate trees in clusters among the leaves. In order to fertilize the female tree, one must climb the male tree and get some of its flowers. One then ascends the female tree and ties among its flowers a bunch of the pollen-bearing male flowers.[12]

Thus, to climb the palm tree is to fertilize it. Solomon is using some contemporary language of the vineyard to say he intends to make love to Shulamith right away!

Solomon says he will caress her fruit stalks—her breasts. Now he changes images from date palms to grape clusters for breasts, which seems more appropriate. Grapes swell and become increasingly round and elastic as they ripen, similar to the female breasts when sexually aroused.

7:9 SOLOMON: And the fragrance of your breath like apples,
And your mouth like the best wine.

Her mouth is "like the best wine." In other words, it is a great source of pleasure. Her kisses are "sweeter than wine."

7:9 SHULAMITH: It goes down smoothly for my beloved
Flowing gently through the lips of those
who fall asleep.

To what does "it" refer? Obviously, it goes back to the "wine," or high sexual pleasure. She says her love is totally and completely satisfying to him—"it goes down smoothly." She is fully confident of her lovemaking skill and knows she can satisfy her man. As wine causes the body to relax and drift into sleep, so their love has left them sweetly exhausted, and they fall asleep in one another's arms.

7:10 SHULAMITH: I am my beloved's
And his desire is for me.

SOLOMON ON SEX

She thrills at the fact that Solomon desires her physically. This refrain has been slightly but profoundly changed from its three previous usages.[13]

2:16 My beloved is mine and I am his
6:3 I am my beloved's and my beloved is mine,
7:10 I am my beloved's and his desire is for me.

This could possibly suggest a deepened sense of security in Solomon's love. When she first mentions the refrain it is during their courtship, and her possession of Solomon is primary, while his possession of her is secondary. The second time she reverses the order, making his possession of her primary, indicating a greater degree of security in him. Now, after this love scene where she has totally satisfied her man, she not only places his possession of her in the forefront, but she strengthens it by saying that his desire is toward her. She is so focused on him that she omits her possession of him. She is revelling in her "woman power" —her ability to satisfy her man physically. The word translated "desire" is the same word used in Gen. 3:16 where it is said the woman's desire would be toward her husband.

They have just consummated sexual union. As they lie there together, Shulamith broaches a subject that has long been on her heart; she desires to visit the countryside and now claims the "vacation for two" Solomon promised her on the honeymoon night (4:8).

7:11 SHULAMITH: Come, my beloved, let's go out into the country,
        Let us spend the night in the villages
7:12   Let us rise early and go to the vineyards;
        Let us see whether the vine has budded
        And its blossoms have opened
        And whether the pomegranates have bloomed.
        There I will give you my love.
7:13   The mandrakes have given forth fragrance
        And over our doors are all choice fruits,
        Both new and old
        Which I have saved up for you my beloved.

In these verses, Shulamith invites Solomon for an escape into the forests of the Lebanon mountains to the north. There, she says, they will make love outdoors! I think any married couple would do well to follow

THE DANCE OF THE MAHANAIM

her advice in planning a few getaways every year where they can renew their physical love and evaluate their marriage and goals in life. My wife and I try to do this at least twice a year. I wish we could do it once a month!

Note, wives, Shulamith suggests this adventure away from the palace. There are places to make love other than the bedroom. Shulamith is suggesting they make love in the open air of the countryside. With a little careful research you can probably find a private spot for you and your mate to enjoy a Sunday afternoon making love out under the sky. Be sure your research is thorough, however, or your picnic for two might suddenly be interrupted by a troop of Boy Scouts tromping through the woods!

Notice she longs to see "whether the vine has budded and its blossoms have opened" (7:12). It is apparently spring. They had courted and were married in the midspring (2:10–14). Perhaps this indicates the passage of one year since their marriage. "The mandrakes have given forth fragrance. . . ." The mandrake was considered an aphrodisiac in the ancient world.[14] To say they give forth fragrance is a poetic way of saying the springtime atmosphere of the countryside is conducive to making love.

When she says ". . . Over our doors are all choice fruits, Both *new* and *old*, Which I have saved up for you my beloved," she is promising both new and old things in their countryside lovemaking. The "doors" refer to the fact that they are outside, and their "doors" are the branches in the trees and the open air. Fruit is a reference to sexual pleasure in general here. Thus, she has saved up some sexual pleasure they are accustomed to, and with the coming of the new fruit of a fresh spring she has some new sexual pleasures she plans to offer him. She is creative! She is skillfully building his sense of anticipation by appealing to his sexual imagination.

> 8:1 SHULAMITH: Oh that you were like a brother to me
> Who nursed at my mother's breasts
> If I found you outdoors, I would kiss you;
> No one would despise me either.

She expresses her desire to be free to unashamedly kiss her husband in public as well as in private. It is all right to kiss your brother unashamedly in public because no one will think of sexual connotations—"no one would despise me either." However, to kiss your husband like that is deemed socially inappropriate. Times haven't changed.

SOLOMON ON SEX

8:2 SHULAMITH: I would lead you and bring you
      into the house of my mother,
      who used to instruct me;
      I would give you spiced wine to drink
      from the juice of my pomegranates.

If you were my brother, she says, we could live at my home in the country. I would feed you from the juice of my pomegranates (from the vineyard of my sexual pleasures), and sit under your instruction as I used to sit under my mother's.

8:3 SHULAMITH: Let his left hand be under my head,
      And his right hand embrace me.

She is now referring to what she said in 7:12, 13. They are going to make love in the country. The momentary daydream of her desire that Solomon be like a brother is broken, and she longs for the opportunity to make love with him in the countryside. She imagines his left hand under her head as she lies on her back in some country meadow, and his right hand "embracing" or "fondling" her breasts and "garden."

For the third time in the book now, Shulamith repeats the warning not to allow sexual passion to develop until God has brought the right man (i.e., the one He wants you to marry) into your life.

8:4 SHULAMITH: I want you to swear, O Daughters of Jerusalem,
      Do not arouse or awaken love,
      Until it pleases.

For the third time she addresses the imaginary chorus with this warning. Let us review the warnings.

First warning, 2:7: If you want to have the maximum sexual joy and fulfillment in marriage, do not allow sexual arousal to occur with anyone but the one God intends for you.

Second warning: If you want to be free to evaluate objectively and to consider the cost of marriage to this particular person, do not allow yourself to become sexually stimulated, or your objectivity may be lost, and there are great issues at stake, 3:5.

Third warning: This one in 8:4 seems to stress the importance of premarital chastity in view of the sexual adjustments to be made "after you've said 'I do.' " To involve yourself sexually before marriage can

THE DANCE OF THE MAHANAIM

hinder your ability to resolve sex problems after marriage. We now know this is not simply theoretical. Any marriage counselor can give numerous illustrations of the effects of premarital sexual involvement on postmarital sexual adjustment.

For example, it often results in premature ejaculation difficulties for the men. The guilt some wives feel over their premarital sexual involvement can so scar their emotions that they continue to think of sex as wrong even in marriage and freeze up sexually. One woman complains of the fact that every time she makes love with her husband, she carries mental images of the other men she had relationships with before she was married. These images generate continued guilt. No, Shulamith's warning is very relevant to the twentieth century. The new morality is just the old immorality that has plagued the lives of many and destroyed numerous marriages over the centuries.

Fortunately, the believer in Christ can experience forgiveness of sin through the cross. Every sin you will ever commit has been paid for if you trust Christ as Savior. What a freedom! "There is therefore now no condemnation to those who are in Christ Jesus" (Rom. 8:1). If God can forgive murder, He can forgive premarital sex. Claim that forgiveness now (1 John 1:9)!

COMMENT

This beautiful love scene and the ensuing conversation suggest several pertinent applications to marriage today.

The Dance of the Mahanaim

As mentioned in the commentary, Shulamith obviously was not very inhibited. To dance like this, provocatively displaying one's body, might seem a little unusual for Western tastes. We must remember, however, that the Bible is a Near Eastern book, and such behavior would not seem at all inappropriate in that cultural context. Furthermore, the fact that Shulamith displayed this kind of freedom doesn't imply that this is a norm for all Western wives. She was being creatively aggressive to please her man within the confines of her own personality and culture. The Bible does not want any woman to try to be something that is totally at variance with her personality. However, it could be that God would have an inhibitied wife change her personality a little and strive to be what her husband needs!

SOLOMON ON SEX

The first thing that would inhibit any wife from this kind of foreplay in the bedroom is concern about her figure. If she thinks she is overweight, she will be very inhibited when it comes to this kind of bedroom behavior. She thinks her husband is only looking at the bulge around the middle. A wise woman once counseled, "Stand nude in front of a mirror and take a good look at yourself. Don't just look at the front; your husband sees the back too. Turn sideways and get a glimpse of what you look like to him." If you think there are some improvements needed, make them!

Many marriage counselors consider inhibitions the number one cause of frigidity in women. Nothing so dramatically surfaces this issue as the contemplation of doing the dance of the Mahanaim for your husband. Perhaps because of our society's perversion of sex, many wives tend to react to the other extreme. In view of so much perverted exploitation of the human female body, it is natural to think that since the world displays it, a wife should conceal it. But certainly inhibition, whatever the causes, can generate considerable sexual tension in a marriage.

Overcoming it is a very difficult thing. It might be helpful to consider that many of our ideas concerning modesty and "virtue" are really not related to the Bible at all. In their book, *The Freedom of Sexual Love*, Joseph and Lois Bird speak directly to this concern. "Nudity between husband and wife has nothing, repeat, nothing, to do with the virtue of modesty. In the intimacy of marriage, undressing for each other should be as natural and unselfconscious as a shared laugh or a mutual prayer."[15]

Shulamith recognizes men are more aroused initially by sight—by a physical approach. Women often approach their husbands in a way they like to be approached—with romance, gentleness, etc. While that is certainly appropriate, it is sometimes a kind of selfish indifference to the husband. On the other hand, husbands sometimes approach their wives in the way they, the husbands, like to be approached. Men tend to be more physical and direct. Wives often say their husbands move too quickly to genital stimulation. The reason they do is that they are selfishly approaching their wives the way that appeals to them, not really thinking of their needs for tenderness and romance. Notice that Solomon always approaches his wife sexually with romance, atmosphere, and tenderness (Song 4:1–8). Shulamith, on the other hand, aggressively approaches her husband in a more physical way—with a dance (Song 7:1–9). Both are concerned with meeting their mate's needs and not insisting on sex on their own terms!

While such a dance would be inappropriate for many marriage relationships, if you and your husband have the kind of freedom and lack of inhibition described here (and there is nothing necessarily wrong if you don't), you might try some of these suggestions. Near Eastern Dancers often wore provocative negligees while dancing. Shulamith did, and she also wore sandals (7:1,2). Thus, sandals and sexy negligees are part of a *biblical* description of foreplay!

The intimate afterwards

Tim LaHaye has pointed out a basic difference in the male and female sex drive cycles. He diagrams it this way:[16]

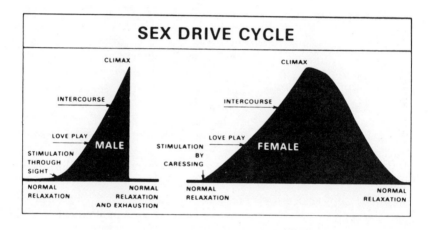

The difference in cycle is beautifully brought out in the Song. After they consummate their love, they fall asleep in one another's arms after engaging in loving conversation (7:9–13). Many husbands fail to express this post-orgasm intimacy and expression of love. This is because, as the diagram indicates, once the man has experienced orgasm, there is an almost immediate return to normal relaxation and even exhaustion. At this point many husbands roll over and go to sleep!

SOLOMON ON SEX

However, it's not over for her. As the diagram indicates, there is a gradual tapering off of her sexual feelings back to normal relaxation. If you are not sensitive to this, your wife can begin to feel taken for granted. "All he wants me for is sex," she may think. Or "The only time he gives me any affection is when he wants sex!" If you roll over and fall asleep as soon as you're satisfied, what other conclusion can she draw?

Paul taught that sexual intercourse was to picture Christ and the church (Eph. 5:31–32). This is an astounding parallel and certainly ought to have forestalled the common notion that Christianity is against sex. What is the essence of the parallel? Death! Paul said the husband was to love his wife as Christ loved the church and *gave Himself* for her. The believer is told that in denying himself and losing his life, he will paradoxically find it (Mark 8:35). Mutual death to self is the key to total oneness spiritually and physically.

To what does the wife need to die in the physical realm? She needs to die to inhibition. Inhibition is sometimes a subtle form of rebellion. Paul says the wife no longer has authority over her own body and the husband no longer has authority over his. Once you are married, you own your mate's body (1 Cor. 7:4). Thus, inhibition is insisting on an authority that you no longer have and thus is sin.

The husband, on the other hand, needs to die to the feelings of embarrassment or awkwardness in expressing tenderness and romance. Both must die for the intimacy of the total oneness of sexual love to be experienced. You both die to anything that would obstruct your mate's pleasure.

Something old and something new

Shulamith is a creative lover. Instead of sitting around resenting Solomon for his preoccupation with his job and his late night approach, she assumes responsibility for her behavior and changes the relationship. First of all she is more aggressive toward him sexually, as illustrated by the dance of the Mahanaim. Then she reveals she has planned a vacation in the Lebanon mountains where they will walk, enjoy the springtime, and make love outdoors. Furthermore, she builds his anticipation of the time together by enticingly suggesting she has something old and something new to offer him. She has planned some new sexual "fruit" or surprises for them to enjoy (7:13).

There are three basic keys to fully satisfying your man sexually.

THE DANCE OF THE MAHANAIM

Be more aggressive

I really think most men long for their wives to be more aggressive sexually. A man wants to know you long for him just as he longs for you. In a survey of 500 men, 39 percent said their biggest dissatisfaction in their sexual relationships with their wives was that their wives were not aggressive enough. Recent books have recommended you call your husband at work and tell him you "crave his body," or that you will meet him at the door when he comes home wearing *only* high heels and jewelry! (If you are shy you can wear lots of jewelry.)

Many people react to this sort of thing and say, "That's just not me!" Then don't do it. Do what *is* you. Ask God to show you what you can do, and be willing to put your inhibitions aside. Just remember to approach him according to the way God designed him, through the eye gate as Shulamith did. If your husband doesn't want you to be more aggressive, then don't be. The goal is to be what your man wants. Know your husband and what he wants, and if what he wants is the dance of the Mahanaim, get on your dancing sandals!

Be totally available

The Scripture plainly says, "The wife's body does not belong to her alone but also to her husband" (1 Cor. 7:4). One doctor was telling a wife that she should be totally available to her husband, and the wife got a look of horror on her face. "If I was totally available to him, we'd never get out of bed!" she said. The doctor assured the distraught patient she and her husband wouldn't have intercourse nearly as often as she expected. He told her, "Someone who bangs on the door forty times when it stays locked, only knocks once if you open right away."

Most wives who haven't reached sexual harmony with their husbands find them making some kind of advance nearly every night. These women are afraid they will be asked to participate more often than they can bear if they let down the barriers. But actually, a man who has intercourse as often as he wants finds that in a week or two the pressure of his physical urge is relieved, and the psychological pressure to overcome resistance no longer applies, so his sexual pace tapers off.

One man explained to me that his wife is available to him in "spurts." After she has read a book about what a wife should be, or heard someone speak on it, or when they have a fight about sex, she has a good attitude for a few days; soon, however, she returns to her old habits of rejection.

He said when she is responsive, "I take advantage of it because I know it won't last long. And because I do, my wife thinks all I ever think about is sex."

You know, when you are on a diet, all you can think about is food. When you can have food anytime you want, you're not nearly so interested. It's the same with sex. When a man or woman knows they will be rejected, they will very likely be consumed with what they can't have. When a man knows his wife is totally available, his desire will gradually decrease. It may take some time, but gradually as he sees you lovingly and eagerly available to be loved by him, the frequency of your love-making will come to a level more acceptable to you.

One woman had a husband who approached her very often, several times a day, including the middle of the night. They had fights; she told him he was oversexed. Finally, he said he had had it and would approach her no more. She called my wife and said, "Linda, I've heard you say publically and privately your goal in life is to be a godly woman. Well, let me tell you, my goal in life is to make my husband scream for mercy!"

The poor man didn't know what had hit him. She told my wife she knew she was succeeding when she approached him sexually while he was watching television and he said, "Please! Let me finish this program." She found she had to prove her total availability to him by being aggressive.

This woman furthermore found her husband was truly satisfied. Sex to a man isn't only physical. When she was warm, responsive, and aggressive to her husband, he felt he was *loved* and not just *endured*! His psychological needs of acceptance, of wanting to be needed, and of wanting total involvement from his wife had been met. As a result his obsession for sex began to diminish. He still was very active sexually, but their relationship was much improved because of her changed attitude.

People do have different amounts of sexual desire. If you are married to a man with a high sex drive, ask God to make your desire equal to his. Perhaps your husband has a low sex drive. It's possible that it is physiological, but it could also be psychological. I know of one case where it was directly related to the fact that the woman was trying to lead the family, and therefore he just wasn't interested in her.

Let's look a little more at the psychological aspects of availability. A man once told me about his wife, "Even when she satisfies me physically, I come away with a need. I feel she hasn't really given or really enjoyed but just put up with me. I need a sexual release again quickly because I guess I'm longing for that total oneness and release that comes when

145

THE DANCE OF THE MAHANAIM

both partners completely give of themselves. I know if I was satisfied physically, emotionally, and spiritually that I wouldn't walk around thinking about sex, wanting it and aching inside."

On the other hand, let's look at it from the woman's point of view. Perhaps she is busily making Christmas presents. The children are finally in bed, and for the first time that day she has a chance to do something she wants and needs to do. While she is totally engrossed, in walks her husband with that special gleam in his eye. At this point she has a choice. She can say, "Oh honey, not tonight," or she can *decide* and choose to love this man God has given her. Even if her initial response is "Oh, no," she can change that immediately to "Oh, yes!"

And once she is in his arms, she has more choices to make. I'm convinced that much of a woman's sexual response is in her brain. If he is kissing her and she is still thinking about the Christmas gifts, she can decide to think about loving him and ask God to give her a desire for him. If she will think and dwell on how nice his body feels and what a privilege it is to love him, the thoughts of the Christmas presents she was making will fade away.

Be creative

A wise woman once said, "You can become a Rembrandt in your sexual art, or you can stay at the paint-by-number stage."[17] The woman who would never think of serving her husband the same frozen television dinner every evening sometimes serves him the same frozen sexual response every night. Sex, like supper, loses much of its flavor when it becomes predictable. It is *biblical* for a wife to be a skillful lover to her husband. Solomon said of Shulamith's love skill, "How beautiful is your love, my sister, my bride! How much better is your love than wine. . . ." He said she was more skilled than any mistress of the empire (Song 6:8). The young man of Prov. 5:19 is told to be drunk with his wife's sexual skill!

What is skill? It's a lot more than technique! It is primarily an attitude of total availability, that is 90 percent of "skill." If a woman has this attitude, she and her husband together can figure out all the "skills" they need without having to read any books. To be "creative" is to bring into existence something that hasn't been there before. Here it applies to bringing into existence a vital and invigorating sexual life. It involves taking the initiative. And finally, it does involve some imaginative new ideas, but they are not nearly as important as the fundamental attitudes

SOLOMON ON SEX

we have been talking about in the preceding chapters of this book.

Where does that leave you? O.K., so I'm supposed to be creative. But what do I do? In chapter 6 we made some suggestions to the men, but for a woman's point of view may I refer you to my wife's excellent book (I'm not at all prejudiced!), *Creative Counterpart* (Thomas Nelson, Inc., 1977) in which she devotes an entire chapter to the subject of the "Creative Lover."

The conclusion of our little song is upon us. We have left our lovers strolling along a country road as they come to Shulamith's home in the Lebanon mountains. As they emerge from the forests where they have shared their love, Shulamith for the third time warns against the premature arousal of sexual passion (8:4). Her warning that it not be awakened until you are committed to your future husband becomes the introductory theme of the book's conclusion. The poet in his final song will direct our attention to the nature of the love Solomon and Shulamith share and how it can be developed.

FOOTNOTES

1. Dr. Otto Zockler, *The Song of Songs (Lange's Commentary*, 12 Vols., Grand Rapids: Zondervan, 1960), V, 115.

2. See Lehrman, p. 25 and Delitzsch, p. 122.

3. Delitzsch, p. 122.

4. William Gegenius, *A Hebrew and English Lexicon of the Old Testament*, ed. Brown, Driver, & Briggs (London: Oxford University Press, 1966), p. 1057.

5. Robert Gordis, *The Song of Songs* (New York: The Jewish Theological Seminary of America, 1954), p. 93.

6. Rabbi Dr. S. M. Lehrman, *The Song of Songs* (The Five Megilloth, ed. Dr. A. Cohn; New York: The Soncino Press, 1946), p. 26.

7. S. Craig Glickman, *A Song for Lovers* (Downers Grove: InterVarsity, 1976), p. 83.

8. Ibid., p. 84.

9. *Hastings Dictionary of the Bible*, ed. James Hastings (5 Vols; Edinburgh: T&T Clark, 1910), III, 656.

10. *International Standard Bible Encyclopedia*, ed. James Orr (4 Vols.; Grand Rapids: Eerdmans, 1939), IV, 2236.

11. *New Bible Dictionary*, J. D. Douglas, ed. (Grand Rapids: Eerdmans, 1962), p. 1294.

12. *International Standard Bible Encyclopedia*, IV, 2235.

13. Craig Glickman, "The Unity of the Song of Solomon," (Dallas Theological Seminary: Th.M. Thesis, 1974), p. 48.

14. Delitzsch, p. 1, 6.

15. Joseph and Lois Bird, *The Freedom of Sexual Love* (Image Books, Doubleday & Co., 1970), p. 104.

16. Tim LaHaye, *How To Be Happy Though Married* (Wheaton: Tyndale House, 1968), p. 64.

17. Marabel Morgan, *The Total Woman* (Old Tapan, New Jersey: Fleming H. Revell, 1975).

CHAPTER TEN
A VACATION IN THE COUNTRY

(Reflection #14, Song 8:5–14)

CONTEXT

One mark of a good writer is his wisdom in selection of his material. In portraying this love story, our poet could have used many incidents in the lives of Solomon and Shulamith. The fact that out of many possible experiences he selects the ones he does naturally leads us to ask, "Why?"

He selects material in order to accomplish his purpose. He has something to tell us and chooses to do it without directly telling us what he wants to say—by stringing a series of reflections (small love songs) together in such a way that a message is revealed. With great artistry, the poet selects several fitting incidents with which to conclude his love song.

Since the theme of love has been the burden of the book, he tells us in the concluding verses how this love can be attained and of what it really consists. The following chart summarizes the poet's craftmanship.

A VACATION IN THE COUNTRY					
LOVE AWAKENED	LOVE DEFINED		LOVE DEVELOPED		LOVE ENJOYED
WHEN: under the apple tree 8:5	it is . . . INTENSE 8:6 8:7a	it is . . . INVALUABLE 8:7b	by . . . a caring family 8:8 8:9	by . . . responsible choices 8:10 8:12	"Hurry, my beloved" 8:13 8:14

COMMENTARY

Love awakened

In the preceding reflection, Shulamith had spoken of a vacation in the Lebanon mountains. As this reflection opens, we find the royal couple walking down a country road. Shulamith has just warned, for the third time, against the premature awakening of love's passions (8:4). As the poet allows us to eavesdrop on their conversation, the theme of the timing of her sexual awakening is discussed.

> 8:5 CHORUS: Who is this coming up from
> the wilderness
> Leaning on her beloved?

Apparently, Solomon and Shulamith have just come from the forest where they shared their love. They are now at peace and their love has been reconfirmed. The chorus provides a transition into the next scene.

> SOLOMON: Beneath the apple tree I awakened you
> There your mother was in labor with you
> There she was in labor and gave you birth.

The text associates the apple tree here with Shulamith's home and birthplace. Her home may have been shaded by the apple tree to which Solomon referred. Thus, the apple tree does double duty here as a symbol for the awakening of physical life at birth and the awakening of sexual life on the wedding night (to which she had referred in her warning to the daughters in the preceding verse—8:4). By calling the reader's attention to the awakening of sexual passion once again, the poet introduces us to the theme of the last reflection—the development of the love of which the book speaks. Before that can be explained, however, he leads us into her comments about the nature of the love they share which leads her to so commit herself to him.

Love defined

8:6 SHULAMITH: Put me like a seal over your heart
            Like a seal on your arm.

The seal of a king was commonly a sign of his ownership. It signified something of great value. She desires to be set as a seal on her husband's heart—the place of his affection. To be set like a seal on his arm is to be in the place of his strength or protection. Why does she desire to be placed as a seal on his heart and arm? The basis for her request is found in the following verses. As long as she resides there (near his heart) she knows the love of the king will keep her and give her security. This is because his love is "as strong as death," and beyond purchase; it is invaluable.

(1) *Love is intense.* She wants to be near his heart always, because she first of all knows the intense nature of his love for her.

> For love is as strong as death
> Jealousy is as severe as Sheol;
> Its flashes are flashes of fire
> The very flame of the Lord.

His love is like death because of its finality and irreversibility. Frequently in the Old Testament, God is presented as jealous in His love for His people, Israel. To say God is "jealous" simply means he has intense love and concern. He desires Israel's exclusive devotion to him and not to other gods. In a similar way, true love, says the bride, is like this. It is exclusive and it is intense. Such is Solomon's love for her and that is why she desires to be near his heart and under his protection.

She even likens Solomon's love for her to "flashes of fire," the very "flame of the Lord." The fire of God's love for His people is often described as an unquenchable fire in the Bible. It burns so intently a river could not put it out.

> 8:7 SHULAMITH: Many waters cannot quench love
> Nor will rivers overflow it;

Certainly "waters" (trials, hurts, problems) will attempt to squelch this love and drown it, but such perfect love cannot be deadened by these factors. Run a river over it and it still burns.

This kind of love, of course, is only rarely (if ever) obtained by fallen men. It is God's ideal.

(2) *Love is invaluable*.

> SHULAMITH: If a man were to give all the riches
> of his house for love,
> He would be utterly despised.

Why would this man be despised? Because he erroneously thinks love can be earned (purchased with riches) or in some way deserved. The poet is not being so obvious as to say that true love can't be bought with money. That was clearly known. He is emphasizing the fact that worthwhile love is never earned, but can only be freely given. If you set a price of a million dollars on it, it still couldn't be purchased. It comes the same way God's love for us comes—when it is freely given. Like the riches of Christ, such love is invaluable. A love that is "freely given" creates a sense of security in the one loved. If the person being loved senses he must earn or deserve love, he or she lives on a performance standard. Solomon did not put his wife on a performance basis. She knew she was loved regardless of how she behaved.

How is this ideal love to be obtained? It is to this question that our mind naturally wanders after such a glowing and beautiful description of committed love. While many ingredients are involved, our poet singles out two for special mention. Such love is obtained when one is raised by a caring family and when one makes responsible choices.

Love developed

In order to find satisfactory answers to the question of the source of this quality of love, one must go way back to the beginnings of character development, back to the home. Thus in a kind of "flashback" the poet takes us back to Shulamith's childhood as she was approaching puberty. Of all of the events he could have related to us, he singles out one, a conversation young Shulamith's brothers had among themselves. Apparently, then, we are to see in this conversation something central to the development of intense and unconditional love.

The basis for believing this is a "flashback" is in 8:10 where Shulamith clearly speaks of her adolescence: "I was a wall . . ." referring to her inaccessibility sexually during that time.

> 8:8 BROTHERS: We have a little sister,
> And she has no breasts;
> What shall we do for our sister
> on the day she is spoken for?

Shulamith's brothers are concerned for their sister's future marriage and happiness. They want to prepare her for the "day she is spoken for"—the day of her marriage. At this point, she is without breasts (still entering puberty). Soon she will develop into a mature woman and the boys will begin to call; her brothers want to prepare her for that. Their strategy is simple and wise.

> 8:9 BROTHERS: If she is a wall,
> We shall build on her a battlement
> of silver;
> But if she is a door,
> We shall barricade her with
> planks of cedar.

Their strategy depends on her character. If she is a wall—impervious to the boys' advances—they will simply encourage and praise her for her virtuous stand. To place a battlement of silver on a wall is to decorate it to make it more beautiful. Just as this battlement of silver increases the beauty of the wall, they will attempt to increase her good character by praise.

There is, however, another possibility. It could be that Shulamith will turn out to be a door—easily entered, easily seduced. Should that prove to be the case, they will take a different approach. They will barricade her with planks of cedar. In other words, they will be very strict with her and protect her from the boys' advances.

SOLOMON ON SEX

In essence the brothers were committed to a little of both approaches. Surely they would praise her, and surely they would restrict and protect her when necessary. Encouragement and discipline were the characteristics of this caring home. Such things take love and time and careful attention. Yet the poet singles out this kind of an environment as one factor in Shulamith's ability to develop an intense and unconditional love for her husband.

But there is more. No matter what kind of home environment one is provided with, he must begin to make responsible choices regarding his sexuality that represent his own values and not simply those of his parents. Shulamith informs us she made such responsible choices in the following verses.

> 8:10 SHULAMITH: I was a wall, and my breasts
> were like towers;
> Then I became in his eyes as one
> who finds peace.

It was unnecessary for her brothers to build a plank of cedar around her; she chose to be a wall. And when she matured, her breasts were "like towers." The towers on the walls of the city were the first things an enemy saw. But because of the ability of the tower to provide a defense for the wall and the city, the sight of those towers discouraged an attack.

In a similar way, Shulamith's fully developed breasts, ready for love, were inaccessible. She was impressive to look at, like the towers of the city, and was one of the first maidens to be seen (due in part to her lovely figure). But any enemy of her virtue was quickly repelled.

The next phrase is emphatic in the Hebrew: "THEN I became in his eyes as one who finds peace." When? After deciding to be a wall. As a result of assuming responsibility for her virtue, she found favor in "his eyes" (Solomon's). The phrase seems to be a play on words. The Bible uses a similar expression for a man finding grace in the eyes of the Lord (Noah). She is saying she found grace, favor in Solomon's eyes. The idea is that Solomon fell in love with her.

But why was the normal biblical usage of finding "grace" changed in this instance to finding "peace." Her name, when pronounced out loud, sounds like "Shulamith." Solomon's name in the original Hebrew sounds like "Shulomoh." The Hebrew word for peace is "shalom." Thus, she says, "*Shulamith* had found *shalom* with *Shulomoh*." She found love and romance when she found Solomon. Her responsible behavior for her own sexuality revealed a character that was able to attract the king's love.

The theme of responsible choices, freely made (not forced by her brothers) is now elaborated more fully in a parable of a vineyard.

8:11 SHULAMITH: Solomon had a vineyard at Baal-hamon;
He entrusted the vineyard to caretakers;
Each one was to bring a thousand
shekels of silver for its fruit.
8:12 My very own vineyard is at my disposal;
The thousand shekels are for you, Solomon,
And two hundred are for those
who take care of its fruit.

Shulamith now takes us back to the time she and Solomon first met. Solomon owns many vineyards all over Palestine, and one is located in the north of Palestine at Baal-haman near Shunem, her home town. It was customary for the owner of a vineyard to lease it out. In return for their work, those to whom it was leased received 20 percent of the total profit. In this case the vineyard that belongs to Solomon is leased to Shulamith's brothers; hence it becomes a fitting analogy of Shulamith's person who was also, for a time, under the care and protection of her brothers.

Shulamith often refers to herself as a vineyard (1:6, 2:15) and earlier complains about the workload imposed on her by her brothers that had kept her from tending her own vineyard—her feminine charms—1:5. As Solomon's vineyard had been entrusted to Shulamith's brothers, so was Shulamith. After caring for the vineyard, the brothers produced a 1,000-shekel profit for their king. But the "profit" they produced for Solomon in their care for Shulamith was even greater, and she feels they deserve a reward. Thus when she says, "My very own vineyard is at my disposal," she is asserting that their work is done and she now discharges her person, freely, to whom she desires. Her vineyard is now under her authority and control, and she freely gives of herself to her lover, the king. In the analogy, her way of saying she gives *all* the profits of her brothers' care to Solomon is by saying, "The thousand shekels are for you, Solomon." That is, the entire profit of the vineyard shd gives him. However, since caretakers of a vineyard received 20 percent of the profit, she asks Solomon to give her brothers 20 percent of 1,000 shekels, or 200 shekels, for their efforts in preserving her "fruit" for the king alone. It is probably not a request for literal money, but simply that they be remembered and appreciated.

SOLOMON ON SEX

Thus, not only did her brothers protect her and prepare her to make personal choices when she came of age, she made them responsibly. The poet, then, by selecting these two scenes, tells us something of the development of an intense and unconditional love. It is, first of all, usually rooted in a home in which love is coupled with discipline. Secondly, it is a result of responsible behavior and is freely given. Throughout the Song, both lovers illustrate beautifully the principle of giving freely and of assuming responsibility for their own actions.

But now the conclusion of our love story has come. As it began with a longing for sexual embrace (1:4) it is fitting that it ends with the enjoyment of love.

Love enjoyed

As the lovers prepare to leave Shulamith's country home, Solomon turns to his beloved and whispers:

8:13 SOLOMON: O you who sit in the gardens,
               My companions are listening for
                  your voice—
               Let me hear it.

The Hebrew text does not have the word "My" in front of "companions;" it just reads "companions." It certainly doesn't refer to Solomon's companions, as that would make little sense. The "companions" refer to those who knew Shulamith as a friend and keeper of the vineyard. The playmates of her youth long to hear her speak a farewell.

But while her old friends desire to hear her say something, Solomon says there is something he wants to hear from her also. She understands what he is getting at and playfully turns to him and says, privately, so no one can hear,

8:14 SHULAMITH: Hurry, my beloved,
               And be like a gazelle or a young stag
               On the mountain of spices.

The figures of a young stag and a gazelle picture playfulness and sexual potency. The mountains of spices refer to the "mound of myrrh and hill of frankincense" (4:6)—her perfumed breasts and garden. Thus she invites Solomon to make love.

COMMENT

The senior panic

As a college student I recall the fears that came upon many of the seniors on campus as they faced graduation and the assumption of responsibilities in the real world. We used to call it "senior panic." However, the phrase was often used humorously of girls who came to college for the purpose of getting husbands and who now, as seniors and without any prospects in sight, were going to be thrust out into society minus that anticipated mate. In some cases the "panic" became rather amusing as girls would woefully lament that now that they had arrived at the ripe old age of twenty-two, they had lost their chances for marriage.

In a more serious vein, what of the woman who is widowed or divorced, left with several children and anxious to remarry, but due to age and circumstances feels her opportunities are slim?

In many respects Shulamith faced a similar situation. While all the other girls were caring for their own vineyards and out meeting boys, she had been forced into relative seclusion by her brothers, working all day in the vineyards under the scorching sun. How unlikely that such a girl would ever end up married to the king of the nation! Yet the God who plans our lives causes all things to work together for good. The lesson is this: no matter how impossible the circumstances, God has no problem bringing a future mate, selected by Him, into your life. You may be shut up in the back of an office, forty years old, with four kids to care for. Yet the Lord can bring the right person into your secluded "vineyard" at the appropriate time. Can you trust Him for that?

"Freely given" love

The last section of the book (8:8–12) is really an answer to the question, "How can this love be attained?" She has specified in 8:7 that it cannot be purchased; how then is one to acquire it? Her answer is twofold. First of all, she says it cannot be demanded or deserved; it must be freely given. This, as explained in the commentary, seems to be her meaning when in 8:12 she says, "My very own vineyard is at my disposal." I am not under obligation, but I give freely, she says.

Too many couples think they *deserve* their mate's love. Too many men adopt the attitude that since they provide a paycheck and a home and security, their wives owe them love in return. Little do they realize a

SOLOMON ON SEX

wife doesn't define love in terms of a paycheck, but rather as a total relationship.

What is involved in this "freely given" love? It appears Shulamith has come to this conclusion through experiences she has described earlier in the book. How is love attained? Answer: by freely giving to one another in the midst of problems and not insisting on one's own way. Their love was attained by growth through trials. Their struggles and their personal decisions to freely give of themselves during their struggles knit them together in a deeper bond of love.

Specifically, what did they "freely give?" As we observed in Chapter 9, they did two things. They both assumed responsibility for their own behavior and did not focus on their mate's error. We saw Shulamith choosing to change her attitudes about Solomon's late-night approach to sex and his preoccupation with his job. Instead of sitting around sulking about how neglected and taken for granted she was, she committed herself freely to increasing her own sexual desire and thinking on her husband's positive qualities (5:9–6:3). Furthermore, she changed her actions by aggressively taking the initiative in their sexual love (7:1–9).

The second thing they both freely gave in the midst of their struggles was blessing for insult (1 Pet. 3:9). We see this clearly in Solomon's responses to her continual rejection of his late-night approaches. He praises her exactly as he did on the wedding night and loves her unconditionally (6:4–10)! Thus, they freely gave of themselves in two ways; they assumed resonsibility for their own behavior, and they rendered blessing for insult.

Many would like to experience the kind of love described by Shulamith in Chapter 8. Yet few are willing to pay the price, and end up in the divorce courts blaming each other or "traditional role relationship teachings in the Bible" as the cause. The real cause is something the Bible calls selfishness or sin. Love like this is only fashioned in the anvil of adversity. This type of love is forged in freely choosing to love your mate unconditionally when you are hurt, or when you are having problems in your relationship.

Solomon and Shulamith didn't enter marriage with this kind of love for each other. Their love deepened and grew as they applied God's principles to their problems.

Yours can too!

APPENDIX I
NEW APPROACHES TO SEXUAL DYSFUNCTION

Here, I have attempted to gather some specific information related to two of the most common problems brought into my office for counseling—premature ejaculation and orgasmic dysfunction ("frigidity"). While this material obviously is not derived from an exegesis of the Song of Solomon, it has been so significantly helpful to those with whom I have spoken that I felt it should be included as an appendix to the book. This information has been developed from consultations with gynecologists, counselors specializing in problems related to sexual dysfunctions, my own counseling experience, and readings from some of the more recent medical studies available.

According to numerous studies, half the people reading this material will identify with the factors being discussed. In this country, 50 percent of the marriages are "sexually dysfunctional or imminently so."[1]

It is extremely difficult to reduce problems as complex as these to paper. They really need to be dealt with by a qualified Christian counselor. The problem is that so few counselors are available. Dallas, for example, with a population of over one million and an evangelical population larger than any other city in the country, has not one *Christian* counselor that specializes in dealing with sexual problems. Thus, to advise a Christian couple to go see a counselor (as many psychologists reading this section would be prone to do) is like telling a blind man to see; it's impossible! There isn't anyone! Thus, this information must be communicated in written form.

Having said that, some definite guidelines can be charted that, when faithfully applied, can bring relief to many who read this book. If the "steps to solution" outlined here don't seem to work for you, that doesn't at all imply there is something wrong with you; it simply means the interpersonal issues are much more complex than I can relate to on paper. Furthermore, if these suggestions do not help, that by no means implies the problem cannot be solved. So consider these ideas as tentative guidelines, and trust the Lord to use them in your lives as He sees fit.

FOUR GENERAL ATTITUDES TO AVOID

These "attitudes to avoid" have been discerned in the counseling office time and time again.

Avoid "blaming your mate"

Numerous counselors will say that until the couple begins to view the *marriage relationship* as the "patient" instead of one another, no progress can be made. The problem is not yours, or hers, or his; it's your relationship that needs treatment. For example, consider a husband who ejaculates prematurely (before his wife reaches orgasm). His wife is not quite sure what to do. If she is aggressive toward him, he might withdraw because he fears the "failure" associated with another sexual encounter. Communication barriers begin to develop. Now, as a result of the scars built by submerged communication, they not only have the problem of premature ejaculation, but that very problem has been made incapable of solution because of the communication tensions. Obviously, the interpersonal interactions of all sexual problems play an enormous part in the cause and solution to sexual problems.

So, stop thinking *he* has a problem or *she* has a problem; it should be *WE* have a problem. This is part of what Paul meant when he said,

In the same way husbands ought to love their wives as their own bodies. He who loves his wife loves himself. After all, no one ever hated his own body but he feeds and cares for it, just as Christ does the church—for we are members of His body. For this reason a man will leave his father and mother and will be united to his wife, and the two will become one flesh. This is a profound mystery, but I am talking about Christ and the church. However, each one of you also must love his wife as he loves himself, and the wife must respect her husband (Eph. 5:28–33).

You see, your mate's problems are your problems because you are one, just like Christ and the church. The proper attitude is, "Let's both of us go to a counselor and see if we can get some insight into *our* problem."

Avoid the "spectator role"

This is one of the most damaging barriers to sexual stimulation. Instead of getting totally involved physically with one's mate, forgetting everything else and just "letting" sexual arousal happen naturally, a person may mentally set himself apart and observe his own responses. A person adopts this role because he or she is afraid of failing to respond, and as a result, all stimulation is blocked.

Thus, a couple struggling with the problem of an impotent husband is handicapped because he is continually standing outside the situation looking to see if he is able to get an erection. Decide to stop worrying about your response and simply lose yourself in the pleasures of sharing your mate's love.

Avoid goal-oriented performance

Too frequently, couples set the overcoming of particular problems as the goals of their sexual encounters. This creates a fear of failure—will I achieve my goal? If a wife has never had an orgasm, the goal of sex may become her achievement of that. Every encounter is entered into with the attitude, "Will we fail again?" This fear of failure is the greatet barrier to success.

The man who cannot maintain an erection has fears every time he approaches his wife sexually. He is completely distracted by the thought that he might not have an erection. This worrying about an entirely involuntary process is worse than useless. The wife worries she might make it worse.

SOLOMON ON SEX

The wife who can't achieve orgasm often expects her husband to "do something." He doesn't know what to do. He asks himself why he can't satisfy her and worries so much about his own performance that he can't relax.

As will be discussed later, a major step in solving any sexual problem is to structure special sessions where it is understood by both husband and wife before the lovemaking session begins that nothing is expected.

Avoid myths

Many myths about sexuality are often involved in sexual problems. The only way to avoid them is to become sexually informed.

For example, some believe a "peak" or "explosive" orgasm is normal for all women. This is simply not true.

Unfortunately, many men still embrace the myth that penis size has something to do with their being able to sexually satisfy their wives. It actually has nothing to do with it. After all, the vagina can accommodate the head of a baby! The issue in satisfying your wife is not the size of the penis, but how you use it.

Another myth is that simultaneous orgasm is the normal or even the best way to have sexual intercourse. Miles reports in his surveys that only 13.7 percent of the couples regularly experience simultaneous orgasm.[2] It is extremely difficult, if not sometimes impossible, to time responses that are basically involuntary. There can be just as much joy and self-giving love involved in a husband first of all stimulating his wife to orgasm and then her satisfying him, or vice versa.

PREMATURE EJACULATION

One evening after speaking at a seminar on marriage, a young woman came up to ask about a problem in her sexual relationship with her husband. She had been married five years and had never had an orgasm. In most cases this problem has psychological causes, so I began to ask her some standard questions to see if I could discern the root difficulty. It turned out that she didn't seem to have any psychological difficulties with sex. She thoroughly loved sex and was very much in love with her husband. She had no bad attitudes that she was aware of, and she just couldn't explain it.

Finally, after some fifteen minutes of discussion, it occurred to me to

NEW APPROACHES TO SEXUAL DYSFUNCTION

ask her how long intercourse lasted. She paused, thought for a moment and said, "I think about thirty seconds."

She thought something was wrong with her because she couldn't have an orgasm in thirty seconds! Few women can. For most, it takes from five to ten minutes of clitoral stimulation for a climax. About 12 percent require ten minutes or more. On the other hand, 75 percent of men can climax in under two minutes.

During the early years of marriage, most women are usually tolerant and understanding about premature ejaculation. But after a while, a wife's frustration level may begin to rise, and she may begin to resent her husband, feel used, and make accusations, either verbal or implied, about his failure as a man. Each sexual encounter becomes more and more painful emotionally. He tries to delay his climax.

His wife, on the other hand, has no confidence in his chances for success in the matter and consequently is grabbing, thrusting, and demanding in order to achieve satisfaction before he ejaculates. The friction she causes on the penis and the stimulation of an active and aggressive wife only triggers his orgasm sooner. This may ultimately lead to impotence due to the continual psychological fear of failure. A cycle begins. He won't approach her because he's afraid he'll be premature, and she won't approach him because she doesn't want to be left unsatisfied.

Actually, this is one of the simplest of all sexual problems to resolve. In 97.8 percent of the cases (according to one study), it can be totally eliminated in a matter of weeks.[3] Surprisingly few men are aware of how to achieve control; most fail to realize the basic reasons for the lack.

Often, involvement in premarital sex is a major cause.[4] Premarital encounters are often in the back seat of a car, or in the parents' home, where the emphasis is on getting it over quickly without getting caught. The goal becomes male satisfaction as soon as possible. The result is that in just a few encounters the man learns a selfish approach to sex and sets habit patterns that are reinforced for years in marriage.

A husband should be able to enjoy fifteen minutes of continuous thrusting and be able to build to thirty minutes of actual intravaginal containment (not continuous thrusting). This doesn't necessarily have to characterize every lovemaking session, but you should have this capacity if you and your wife are going to experience all the sensations God intended a husband and wife to enjoy in their love.

Premature ejaculation is defined as the husband's inability to control ejaculation for a sufficient length of time during intravaginal containment to satisfy his wife in at least 50 percent of their times of sexual intercourse.[5]

In the following pages I'll outline the treatment procedure developed by Masters and Johnson that has brought relief to nearly 98 percent of the couples who have applied it.[6]

STEP 1—*Eliminate past myths.*

There are two main myths that hinder solution.

First, it has been taught that because men reach orgasm more quickly, the wife should refrain from direct stimulation of the husband prior to intercourse. The contrary is usually true. A man is more likely to reach orgasm prematurely when he goes *unstimulated* through a long period of preparatory arousal for the woman. Because he becomes so preoccupied with the time for intercourse, anticipation builds to an unbearable degree. Furthermore, through stimulation, the wife can bring him to a sexual peak prior to orgasm that actually reduces the need to climax immediately. Of course, for the wife to refrain from full participation removes the sense of physical intimacy and mutual experience. The whole experience is reduced to getting her ready, entering her, and ejaculating immediately. There is little opportunity for intimacy.

Secondly, the myth that the man is supposed to put his mind on other things needs to be rejected. I've seen Christian books in which the man is instructed to mentally recite Bible verses to get his mind off the pleasure he is experiencing! Others counsel him to worry about business problems. There are two basic downfalls to this "solution." It doesn't work, and it spoils the sense of enjoyment!

STEP 2—*Commit your situation to the Lord as a couple.*

Ask one another's forgiveness for any hurts that may have developed in your marriage because of this problem, then join together in prayer asking the Lord to give you the wisdom and unconditional acceptance necessary to implement these steps. If you are unable to pray about it openly in front of each other, you do not have the necessary acceptance and freedom level to solve the problem. If you can't pray about it, there are some things in your relationship that need to be resolved before you'll be able to work at this. Most sexual problems are either caused by spiritual and relationship problems, or they are made more complicated by these factors.

STEP 3—*Employ the "squeeze technique."*

Agree on a session of sexual stimulation with no goal orientation. There will be no intercourse and no "failure," just mutual sharing of love. The wife should sit at the head of the bed with her legs spread. The husband lies between her legs on his back with his head pointing toward the foot of the bed. His genitals are now close to those of his wife. The

163

wife lovingly and gently caresses her husband's genitals, especially the head of the penis or wherever her husband directs her, to encourage him toward orgasm.

As soon as he approaches orgasm, he gives the signal and she applies the "squeeze technique." She places her thumb on the underside of the penis just where the shaft ends and the head begins (the frenulum). She also places the first two fingers of that same hand on the opposite side of the penis, then squeezes her thumb and first two fingers together with very hard pressure for at least four seconds. She should squeeze as hard as she can. (On an erect penis this will cause no pain.) This pressure will immediately make him lose his desire to ejaculate, and he will lose some of his erection. After fifteen to thirty seconds, she repeats the procedure, manipulating him to full erection again and repeating the squeeze.

STEP 4—*Intercourse in the "woman above" position.*

After learning some control, the husband lies on his back and the wife uses the squeeze technique two or three times: she then straddles him and, leaning forward about 45 degrees, very gently and slowly inserts the penis in her vagina. She should remain motionless—giving her husband a chance to achieve control. If he feels he is going to ejaculate, she merely raises her body and repeats the squeeze procedure, then gently reinserts the penis. After a few sessions of practice in this position, the husband is to thrust just enough to maintain his erection until they can stay in this position for fifteen or twenty minutes before ejaculation. The "male above" position is the most difficult in which to maintain control.

STEP 5—*Intercourse in lateral coital position.*

After control increases, the couple is encouraged to move from this female superior position to the lateral coital position (sideways). Lying on her right side, she leans forward to lie against his chest as she extends her right leg behind her. He bends his left knee, keeping it under her leg and flat against the bed. This position leaves both partners with the greatest freedom and comfort as well as the best ejaculatory control. It has been found that couples who have tried this position use it (by choice) about 75 percent of the times they have intercourse.

STEP 6—*Repetition once a week for six months.*

You should use the squeeze technique at least once a week for the next six months and practice it for about twenty minutes at some time during each of the wife's menstrual periods. Complete ejaculatory control is usually attained in six to twelve months. By this we mean the husband develops control to the point where he can restrain ejaculation indefinitely.

While the couple is learning these steps, it may be necessary for the husband to use manual stimulation or other agreeable means to give his wife sexual fulfillment.

It must be noted here that there often is temporary impotence after the premature ejaculation problem is solved, primarily due to increased frequency of the sex act.

Researchers tell us the squeeze technique is never effective if done by the husband on himself—the wife must be involved.

Even if you are not having problems with premature ejaculation, but you don't have sufficient control to maintain continuous thrusting for fifteen minutes, this technique can be used to build your control up to as long as your wife desires. By making sideways motions with his hips the husband can stimulate his wife's clitoris without bringing any friction on the penis, significantly lengthening the time of intravaginal containment.

ORGASMIC DYSFUNCTION

The most common combination of problems brought up during counseling in regard to sex is premature ejaculation coupled with "frigidity." This inability to climax is the most common sexual dysfunction of women.

It has many causes. Religious background and negative religious attitudes about sex often are major factors. The most common factor is partner dissatisfaction. For some reason she does not respect, trust, or admire her husband. A lack of strong male leadership is often related to the problem. Some women simply have no sense of feeling in their vaginal areas. This is almost always of psychological origin.

There are those who believe an overemphasis on toilet training can be the first step toward orgasmic dysfunction later in life! The little girl may be rushed into toilet training before she is ready, and a big trauma develops over having bowel movements. The little girls begins to think of her genitals as dirty because it was made into such a big deal.

Heavy petting before marriage is a major factor. The "start—stop" pattern is developed. Then she gets married and doesn't know how to keep going.

The double standard of our society which says it's wrong for the female but right for the male often carries over into marriage. A routine and unimaginative approach by the husband often results in orgasmic dysfunction.

Most important, as mentioned earlier, are you a shepherd to your wife?

Does she feel secure and totally accepted? Is there an intimacy of relationship? Are you a leader? Do you communicate strength and tenderness?

In the following pages I will enumerate some steps toward a solution. Let me carefully qualify before I begin. Orgasmic dysfunction is an extremely complex issue and these steps may be helpful to only a few of the wives reading this book. It is impossible to put something this delicate and involved into a series of steps. Every situation is different; every relationship is special.

STEP 1—*Become factually informed*.

Frequently this problem, like so many, is due to lack of knowledge of some very simple physical, psychological, or emotional factors. The best way to become factually informed is to read reliable books. Here are some suggestions.

Understanding Human Sexual Inadequacy, Belliveau and Richter (Bantam Books, Inc., 666 Fifth Ave., New York, N.Y., 10019), QZ5959, $1.25. This excellent little text is a summary of some of the key findings of Masters and Johnson, *Human Sexual Inadequacy (Boston: Little, Brown, and Company, 1970). There are chapters devoted to solutions of all sexual dysfunctions common in marriage: impotence, premature ejaculation, orgasmic dysfunction, painful intercourse, vaginismus, sex in the aging, etc.*

The Freedom of Sexual Love, Joseph and Lois Bird (Image Books, Doubleday & Company, 1970), $1.25. This valuable book is written with the approval of the Catholic church. It is generally Biblically based and is very frank and specific.

Physical Unity in Marriage, Shirley Rice (Tabernacle Church of Norfolk, 7120 Granby Street, Norfolk, Virginia 23505), $1.75. This book, a sequel to *The Christian Home, A Woman's View*, is loaded with practical biblical and medical counsel. The book grew out of a series of lectures Mrs. Rice has given around the country.

Sexual Happiness in Marriage, Herbert J. Miles (Zondervan, 1967), $1.25.

STEP 2—*As a couple, commit your (plural "your") problem to the Lord.*

He is extremely concerned and grieved by the needless pain and tension this has caused your marriage. He desires to help. Open, frank prayer together about this issue will do much to open up communication channels and bring the spiritual dimension to bear on the situation. James says, "You do not have because you do not ask God" (James 4:2).

STEP 3—*Re-establish communication.*

There must be a total freedom of discussion between you on sexual matters. "And the man and his wife were both naked and were not ashamed" (Gen. 2:25). There was no shame in Adam and Eve's sexual relationship; there were no inhibitions.

If there are communciation barriers developing in your marriage over a problem, several things might help open them up. Take the text of the Song of Solomon printed out in Appendix II of this book. The husband should read the parts of Solomon, the wife the parts of Shulamith and the chorus. As you read, stop and comment on any items in the commentary that strike you as points for discussion. Then move on to the next verse. Use the Word as the basis for your discussion!

STEP 4—*Discern and overcome any negative feelings toward men.*

Frigidity is like a log jam on a narrow stream, says psychiatrist Marie Robinson.[7] When two or more logs jam up, all the rest of the logs are blocked and cannot flow down the stream. A gigantic jam stacks up behind the two logs. The emotional problems, hurts, and communication barriers of frigidity are like that jam. When two logs are pulled out, the whole jam begins to flow down the river once again.

The emotional jam we call frigidity is often held in place by two basically negative attitudes. The first is a negative attitude toward men, and the second is a rejection of one's role as a woman.

How can a negative attitude toward men be overcome? Marie Robinson suggests a simple answer, but it takes time. The Scripture says, "As a man thinks in his heart, so is he" (Prov. 23:7). Paul tells the believers in Rome, "Do not conform any longer to the pattern of this world, but be transformed by the renewing of your mind" (Rom. 12:2). Begin by giving yourself some time alone every day. It may be ten minutes, or it may be half an hour, but do it regularly. During these private sessions, explore your inner attitudes toward men. Strive to feel all your negative emotions about your husband. You are advised to "only aim at this point to let these negative feelings come to the surface, to seek them out, experience them to the full."[8] Do this by picking out some small but repeated irritation or annoyance he causes you—the more trifling, the better. Fix on it, then dare to allow your emotions and thoughts about it to become dominant. Do not repress them as you have trained yourself to do over the years.

It needs to be emphasized that it is quite possible you will not have any negative thoughts about men at a conscious level. One woman seemed to be annoyed only at her husband's sloppiness. He left his clothes lying around the house and wouldn't put his shaving cream away after using it in the morning. These were, as far as she was concerned, mere trifles, and weren't worthy of her emotional focus. She had suppressed them for years.

Under counseling, she was encouraged to explore this "trifle" to see if there was anything there. As she allowed herself to feel her irritation fully, she began to uncover a vast log jam of emotional resentment against men in general that she had never been aware of at a conscious level. She interpreted her husband's sloppiness as a symptom of his desire to treat her as a slave and to confine her to demeaning labor. Her anger became more explosive as she continued to reflect on the matter.

It quickly led to her underlying attitude about men in general. All men ever do, she reasoned, is attempt to enslave women and exploit them. All they want from women is sex. Furthermore, they are physically superior and therefore capable of enforcing their demands.

Does your husband's behavior in public embarrass you? Has he any annoying habit? Select some petty things, and allow yourself to feel the full range of emotion that may lurk underneath. In the beginning you are likely to find no very strong feelings or passionate generalizations. But if you persist you will probably find an area where your feelings are indeed intense and negative. These emotions have remained hidden from your subconscious mind for many years because of their emotional intensity.

Most frigid women believe their negative attitudes about men actually represent reality. It is important to realize your investigation is not going to prove your hidden fears to be *valid*, but will prove them *invalid*. And the emotions are *not* overwhelming; therefore, there is no need to fear this emotional exploration process. It is of utmost importance to recognize in advance that whatever emotions turn up are *feelings* and *not reality*.

What good does all this do? One of the major contributions of modern psychiatry has been the establishment of the fact that attitudes and feelings have the power to do lasting harm only when they are hidden from one's awareness.[9] As soon as these negative feelings become fully conscious, they automatically lose the major part of their power to do harm. Once irrational feelings are externalized and can be looked at logically, the drive toward normal psychological health takes over, and release occurs. The next step is to commit them to the Lord and ask Him to remove them from your life.

Furthermore, you must look in Scripture to see the true picture of masculinity. Jesus was very aggressive; he was very courageous; he was a very masculine man. These characteristics, particularly aggressiveness,

168

are not wrong. They do not represent an attack on the female sex or an attempt by men to dominate. They are part of God's design into male biology.

STEP 5—*Deal ruthlessly with any fantasies.*

Some frigid women are dissatisfied with their roles as women. They daydream about various jobs and vocations that are more "valuable" than being wives and mothers. Often they spring from a childhood desire to be an actor, artist, dancer, or concert pianist. Sometimes they concern becoming a corporation president, a doctor, or a lawyer—anything but a beloved wife. These daydreams protect the daydreamer from an inferiority complex. It doesn't matter that she is unable to love: someday (perhaps next year) she will be an actress or a lawyer.

Dr. Robinson suggests the next step in overcoming orgasmic dysfunction is to recognize this daydream for what it is. Let it roll on and on. Dwell upon its glamor. Explore all the details of the fantasy. It will soon become apparent that it is impossible. The dream that has been hidden just below the threshold of consciousness is now totally exposed and seen for what it is—pure childishness. Once the objective factors take over, the dream subsides.

And it must subside because it has become a psychological defense mechanism preventing the frigid woman from surrendering totally to her role as a woman. As long as a woman clings to these impossible notions, the blockage in her emotions prevents her from dealing realistically with life. She is not an actress or a corporation president and God probably doesn't intend that for her. If she is married, God's will for her is to put her husband and children first, and to find her identity and security in total yieldedness to her husband. She must literally "believe and let go" if she is going to experience orgasms.

STEP 6—*Strive for a biblical and positive view of men and the male role.*

The frigid woman tends to fear or resent male dominance and aggressiveness. She views it as a threat or an attempt to exploit her. "All he ever wants is sex," she may say. However, male aggressiveness was built into men by the Creator. Before Eve was created, Adam was given the command to name the animals. In the Hebrew culture, to have authority to name was to have authority over. Thus, Adam named Eve (Gen. 2:23), indicating his authority over her.

Note this was *before* the Fall. Thus, God's original ideal is that the man is in control, and the female is under his authority; this is not an arrangement forced into the course of human affairs because of sin, but is God's

169

original intent. Thus, when your husband takes initiative, when he is competitive, when he is aggressive, he is simply fulfilling his biological destiny built into him by the Creator. It is now a proven fact that there are innate differences between the sexes. The Lord gave man the male hormone, androgen, which is responsible for aggressiveness. Men with a double chromosome tend to be hypermasculine, very tall, aggressive, impulsive, and often violent and delinquent from an early age.[10]

Marie Robinson maintains frigid women must make a re-evaluation of the male sex. These women often have little real knowledge of what men are actually like. Men seem to be powers, not people. By making a re-evaluation and seeing that male aggressiveness is God-given, she can begin to understand her husband as he is and achieve the ability to love him in all of his uniqueness and individuality.

Because a woman's energies are mainly directed inward, in preparation for motherhood and maintaining a home, she often misunderstands her husband when he takes a neat home for granted. He has invested a major portion of his pride elsewhere—in his work. He is doing the business to which God has called him. His sloppiness does not indicate his indifference to his wife; however, the frigid woman will often interpret it that way. He is rejecting her sphere as unimportant, she reasons.

The sex act itself most typically represents male aggression. The thrusting of the penis becomes offensive to the frigid woman. To a normal woman this is of course highly desirable, but the frigid woman can personalize it as an act of aggression by men against women.

She is antagonistic to aggression and does not understand it. His strength and ability to master her environment makes her feel drab. If men were out to enslave women, women could be justified in fearing, hating, and envying man's central strength and aggressiveness. But is he? Once a woman examines this central point, her whole basic attitude can be changed.

Consider the burden upon the average male. In the name of love, he sets his personal freedom aside and marries, thereby taking on the responsibility to provide. He shoulders full responsibility for his wife and children.

As a woman, think for a moment how you would feel if your child were suddenly deprived of food, shelter, and clothing. Generally, these thoughts are only casual passing thoughts to a woman, but a man carries them daily. Every morning he realizes his success or failure in business determines his family's happiness and security. Women, unless they are very close to their men, do not realize how seriously the average husband

SOLOMON ON SEX

takes this responsibility. The responsibility at times becomes enormous. The competition in the market place today is increasing. The economy is unstable. Every man knows if he falters in his job, he can be easily replaced. Few women could take the daily strain the average man assigns to himself when he signs the marriage contract.

Consider your husband's aggressiveness in light of the tremendous duties and responsibilities God has placed upon him. He is responsible before God to rule and have dominion over the planet. He is responsible to provide for his own: "If anyone does not provide for his relatives, and especially for his immediate family, he has denied the faith and is worse than an unbeliever" (1 Tim. 5:8).

As you consider your husband's aggressiveness in this light, you can see it is a necessary part of him if he is to fulfill these responsibilities. Then you are able to feel admiration instead of anger, resentment, or envy. Far from seeking to enslave women through their strength, husbands use that strength and aggressiveness for just the opposite reason—to protect and care for their loved ones. He makes it safe for you to be feminine, to bear children with a sense of security, and to raise them. You know he is always watching over you, protecting you, and is terribly anxious about your safety and happiness. By looking at the end to which male aggression is directed when it matures, can any woman honestly hold such resentment? The same male aggression that initiates the sexual act is the aggression that protects her, provides for her, and allows her to be a wife and mother.

Frequently his male ego, his sloppiness, his irritableness, his slackness are simply the outlets for a day "on the hunt." He doesn't necessarily tell you of all his humiliations, defeats, and things that upset him during the day because he doesn't want to burden you with them. If you see him in this light, it will be difficult to harbor any deep-seated resentments.

STEP 7—*Surrender to your role.*

It should be clear by now that a central thesis of this book is that there is an immediate connection between the Bible's role relationship teachings and a woman's capacity to experience orgasm in marriage. May I now suggest that an approximate synonym for "frigidity" is "lack of submission"! Furthermore, an approximate psychological synonym for "orgasm" is "yieldedness." It was encouraging to me to see a secular psychiatrist, Marie Robinson, making the same observations.

There are two basic logs in the emotional log jam that prevent normal orgasm in women. The first is a negative attitude toward men, coupled with envy of their role and what it would be like if wives could live out their

NEW APPROACHES TO SEXUAL DYSFUNCTION

fantasy roles. The second major log jam is role reversal.

Once these two logs are removed, the whole river begins to flow naturally and all of a woman's basic emotional and spiritual drives will push her into normal orgasm. Of course, many women who rebel at the idea of submission and are quite hostile to men nevertheless do experience an orgasm of sorts. But it is a surface physical release, not the full-throbbing, deep-seated convulsion involving the total body, soul, and spirit that is the biological and spiritual destiny of the totally yielded woman. Furthermore, there are many outwardly submissive, feminine women who either never experience orgasm or who experience a surface orgasm on the level of mere physical release. However, may I advise these women to seriously consider their inner feelings toward men and to inquire into their understanding of total submission and what it means practically.

In a word, the biblical definition of total submission is "no resistance." Resistance is like logs in the emotional jam that block the emotional flow of the river. Dr. Robinson explains:

> As the woman who has suffered from frigidity explodes her groundless fears one by one and explores a new attitude toward men, toward love, toward motherhood, feels a new esteem for her husband—all these things happen, her lifelong *restlessness* begins to depart. For the first time she realizes just how restless she has been, how unsatisfied she feels, how precariously balanced her life, inwardly and outwardly, has always felt. Now something deep within her relaxes, lets down. When this happens, she is beginning to experience the essential attribute of all that is truly feminine, spiritual tranquility.[11]

The Women's Liberation Movement will, perhaps more than anything else, increase the very problem its leaders think they will solve—this inner female restlessness and lack of a sense of fulfillment. Betty Friedan calls it the "problem that has no name." Since nearly 40 percent of American women do not regularly experience orgasm, and since that experience is related to biblical teachings on role relationship, the Women's Liberation Movement falsely concludes that biblical role relationship was the cause of the "restlessness." Just the contrary—it is the failure to apply the role relationship teachings of the Bible that has caused the "problem that has no name." It's the male failure more than the female, but the Bible is not the problem; it's the failure of human beings to apply its principles.

It's sad that a few upper-class female intellectuals have been given a platform to project their own personal problems onto all American

SOLOMON ON SEX

women. Most American women have no problems with the notion of role relationship in theory because they sense that God built these concepts biologically and genetically into male and female relationships. The application of the role relationship is generally complicated by the failure of men to assume a shepherd's role.

For a woman, full orgasm requires a total trust in her partner. The full physical experience is so intense there is a momentary loss of consciousness. She feels as though she's hanging from the edge of that three-story building and is instructed to "believe and let go." She can't do it unless she trusts completely.

Do you as a husband provide that atmosphere of trust and security by assuming responsibility for her, protecting her, and demonstrating self-giving love? Sometimes men tend to be so thoughtful and considerate of their "wife's problem" that their lack of firmness is interpreted as passivity and a lack of masculine strength which can cause her to lose respect and trust.

In sexual intercourse, as in life, man is the actor and the woman is the one acted upon. To give oneself in this passive manner involves total trust. Any vestige of hostility, or fear of one's role, will clearly show in the sexual embrace.

You must be more than *willing* to submit to your husband in general. There must be a genuine *excitement* about the act of surrender pictured in sexual intercourse itself. There must be an *eagerness* to surrender. Have you ever wondered why Paul taught that sexual intercourse was intended by God as a portrait of Christ and the church? He says of the one-flesh relationship (sexual relationship), "This is a profound mystery—but I am talking about Christ and the church" (Eph. 5:32).

The church submits totally to Christ. Indeed, the individual believer *eagerly* submits to Christ, and the result is what? Peace, joy, emotional freedom and release, new love and all of the fruits of the Spirit. Sex is to picture that same total submission by the wife and total protection and love by the husband.

In light of this discussion, let's consider 1 Pet. 3:1-6.

3:1 Wives, in the same way be submissive to your husbands so that, if any of them do not believe the word, they may be won over without talk by the behavior of their wives, when they see the purity and reverence of your lives.

A common problem then, as well as now, is a believing woman

173

married to an unbelieving husband. Notice, Peter says he is to be won to Christ "without talk" (without any preaching), but by godly behavior. One aspect of the behavior is a "submissive" attitude.

3:3 Your beauty should not come from outward adornment, such as braided hair and the wearing of gold jewelry and fine clothes.
3:4 Instead, it should be that of your inner self, the unfading beauty of a gentle and quiet spirit, which is of great worth in God's sight.

The arrival of this gentle and quiet spirit results directly from the fact that a woman really allows herself to trust her husband (no resistance) in a very deep sense. This inner spirit is exactly the opposite of Betty Friedan's "problem that has no name" or the restlessness of American women. Feminine tranquility of spirit is a very precious thing to God. The only other time He uses the phrase "great worth" is in reference to the precious blood of Christ.

The frigid woman can trust no man. Consequently, her approach to life is very painful and difficult. She feels responsible for everything. She certainly can't just let go and trust her husband to take care of it! Details overwhelm her. She has to fight her feelings and resentments about her role just to get routine housework done.

The biggest obstacle to submitting totally is fear. Peter notes this concern in verses 5 and 6.

3:5 For this is the way the holy women of the past who put their hope in God used to make themselves beautiful. They were submissive to their own husbands
3:6 like Sarah, who obeyed Abraham and called him her master. You are her daughter if you do what is right and do not give way to fear.

Notice the last word, "and do not give way to *fear*." If some of you men are wondering why your wives don't seem to support you, but instead always compete with you, they may be afraid of what will happen if they let go completely. That fear that no one will take care of them, that no one will assume responsibility, carries over into the marriage bed. It can be a major reason for her inability to have orgasms. She is afraid to trust you completely because she suspects you might do something similar to what Abraham did to Sarah.

In his fear for his own life, he told his wife to sleep with a foreign king (Genesis 20). Note, however, that Sarah obeyed Abraham, and God

174

intervened. God does not always intervene, and if it had come to sleeping with that king, Sarah should have disobeyed her husband. But she obeyed him and trusted God, and as a result God protected her where her husband failed.

Here is the tremendous advantage the Christian woman has over the non-Christian woman in overcoming the problems of inability to achieve orgasm. The Christian woman can place her trust in God, obey her husband, and find a sense of security (to a degree) that would come from trusting one's husband. Hence she can submit totally even when her husband is disobedient to the Word, because her protection comes from God, and He will never fail her. Sarah overcame the fear barrier by realizing her ultimate trust was in God; wives today can do the same.

As an illustration of these principles at work in real life, allow me to share Mary's story with you. Mary is a very intelligent businesswoman. She was phenomenally well-organized and efficient, and was able to run a business with her husband and maintain a good home at the same time. In her marriage she was always the leader. In fact, she and her husband had talked the situation over, and both had agreed she was more competent and should be the leader.

It was her goal in life to be the president of her own corporation. She hated the word submission and was in constant competition with her husband. She wanted to do the best, do the most, and insisted on her own ideas. Surprisingly, for thirteen years of marriage they had a very good relationship and genuinely loved each other. Their communication was good and their love was deep. However, in the sexual area, their marriage was in jeopardy. She had never been able to have a climax. They were relatively wealthy, and could afford extensive psychological counseling. They flew to more than twenty states and had numerous sessions with many doctors and counselors. Nothing seemed to work. Finally, she found Christ, and a new life began.

Shortly after her conversion, she attended a marriage seminar for women my wife teaches around the country. There, for the first time, she understood the beauty of role relationship as portrayed in the Bible. All the false notions were removed, and she was able to eagerly submit to her new role. Here is an excerpt from one of her letters:

> It seems incredible to me that Jesus has given me so much in life . . . then to dump all of this joy on me is overwhelming. Since your seminar, He's made it so easy for me, maybe knowing that I had the farthest to go, knowing that I had to change every fiber, every attitude I'd developed for

NEW APPROACHES TO SEXUAL DYSFUNCTION

thirty-three years. Only He knows how I fought the word "submissive"! Only He knows how I wanted to lead, be the best, do the most, be the perfectionist, show my ideas!! My giant ego. Now he's given me a new plan and a new purpose for my life. My only daily goal now is to do whatever pleases Bill. God's plan has taken away my competitiveness, my aggressiveness, and given me the strength to become a whole new person. My husband has become the most wonderful leader you could ever imagine. Our home is so happy, so free of stress, free of tension that everyone who visits can almost see the light that Jesus has turned on in every room. Bill is no longer just part of my life, he's my whole life. My career may have to go . . . if it does, I know my Lord will replace it with something many times more meaningful. Of that, I have not one doubt.

When this family began to implement God's plan, new life flowed. Mary, for the first time in her life, now experiences orgasm regularly in less than three minutes! The turning point was when she decided to surrender. In her case she actually made a contract with God on the day she surrendered. Here is how she worded it:

I, today, Wednesday, November 20, vow to myself, not to suggest, tell, nag, or criticize Bill on how to run his business. I will bite my tongue, leave the premises or whatever necessary, not to give my opinion. My knowing that my opinions are right will be satisfaction enough—no one else need share how smart and terrific I really am. I am now willing to accept his business failure to enforce this rule!!! I will read this each day before I start my work. If I should fail to achieve this goal even twice, I will quit my job, knowing it is a hindrance to my becoming "The Total Woman."

Mary discovered the secret of sexual surrender, and once the emotional log jam was released, the ability to orgasm flowed naturally as a part of her spiritual destiny.

STEP 8—*Overcome inhibitions.*

Besides the psychological blocks mentioned in Step 7, probably the second biggest emotional barrier to achieving orgasm is inhibition. Most women come into marriage with a fair share of inhibition, and a marriage license doesn't automatically take that away. These inhibitions can block the freedom of total emotional release.

Inhibitions not only plague the nonorgasmic woman, they stifle the orgasmic woman as well. They are frequently the cause of much tension and resentment on the part of the husband. Often a wife desires to be otherwise, but hasn't the faintest idea how to deal with the problem.

SOLOMON ON SEX

The first step in removing inhibitions is the renewal of the mind. You must saturate your mind with God's viewpoint on sex. If you have read this far, you have already begun that process. But it's not enough just to read in order to have our minds transformed. It needs to be saturated with Scripture. "Do not conform any longer to the pattern of this world, but be transformed by the renewing of your mind" (Rom. 12:2). Because the world tends to flaunt the body and sex, it is natural for Christians to associate inhibition with Christian modesty and the "sacredness" of sex. Actually, based on the Song of Solomon and the rest of the Bible, inhibition *outside* marriage reflects Christian modesty but *within* marriage reflects the pattern of this world. The world system cheapens and degrades sex, but paradoxically, within marriage many women are still inhibited. Because the world exploits the female body to the ultimate, some Christian women desire to be the opposite of the world. The world exposes the body, so they conceal it. They are not going to be like the nasty women in the *Playboy* centerfold and reveal their bodies to their husbands or do the things "those girls" do.

In order to saturate one's mind with Scripture, it must first be memorized. May I suggest you consider memorizing passages from the Song of Solomon or the rest of Scripture relating to sex (1 Cor. 7:1–5; Gen. 2:21–25; Eph. 5:28–33; and especially Prov. 5:15–20). Select passages from the Song that are particularly meaningful to you. Many women have found Song 7:1–9 especially helpful in this regard.

Not long ago my wife counseled a woman who was having severe problems with inhibitions. Every time they made love, the emotional blocks almost paralyzed her from making any kind of positive response. My wife gave her the above advice and told her to memorize some meaningful Scripture from the Song and repeat them to God in prayer all during the week. In the Song, Shulamith reflects on her husband's body (Song 5:10–16). She reflects on their lovemaking experiences (Song 7:1–9; 1:15–2:6; 4:1–5:1). These passages might be a good place for you to start.

My wife told her she was going to call her in one week to have her repeat over the phone all the verses she had memorized. A week later she recited over twenty verses she had memorized and meditated on during the week. When asked how it had helped, she exclaimed, "It's like a miracle; meditating on God's Word has completely released me." She said that while she was making love with her husband the old blocks would sometimes come up. She would immediately meditate on the relevant Scripture passages, and the Word of God would erase the block!

NEW APPROACHES TO SEXUAL DYSFUNCTION

Along with the meditation, it is important to decide in your will that you will be what your particular husband needs physically. We often tend to wait for our feelings. But in the Christian life God wants us to live by our wills. He wants us to make decisions, and then the feelings will follow. So now you must *do* whatever you have had a block about. Don't wait for the inhibitions to somehow just vanish away. Probably the longer you wait, the more inhibited you'll become. It's not going to get any easier.

One woman said that early in their marriage her husband asked her to tell him in detail everything he could do to please her physically, and everything she was going to do to pleasure him.

The embarrassed bride said with a gulp, "In detail?"

And the husband replied, "Yes honey, in *detail*. I would really like you to do that."

She had a choice to make. She could either say to her husband, "That really embarrasses me; I just can't do that." Or she could overcome her embarrassment and do what she knew God wanted her to do—please her husband. The first time she was embarrassed; the second time it got a little easier, and the third time it wasn't very difficult at all.

Give God time to work. It's a process. I've known women who have been released from all inhibitions overnight, but that is the exception rather than the rule. One woman confided that from the time she really knew what God said in Scripture, it took her nearly two years to completely overcome her inhibitions, but it was a steadily upward climb.

STEP 9—*Exercise and develop the P.C. muscle.*

A recent medical discovery has enabled millions of American women to experience orgasm for the first time in their marriages. It all began in the 1940s, when Dr. Kegel, a California gynecologist, was treating female patients for stress incontinence. This problem afflicts many women. It involves the passing of urine accidentally when they laugh or sneeze and can obviously be very embarrassing. Dr. Kegel speculated that the muscle supporting the birth canal and the urinary passage could be the key. Thus he developed a set of exercises for his patients to try to develop and strengthen this muscle. The exercise proved beneficial, and today these exercises, known as the Kegel exercises, are standard technique in cases of stress incontinence.

As his patients began to report their progress, many of them announced something completely unexpected—they were experiencing orgasms for the first time. Kegel was skeptical at first that there could be any connection with the exercises, but the repeated coincidence of improvement in stress incontinence with orgasmic function led him to believe there was something to it.

It is now an established fact that poor muscle tone in this P.C. muscle (pubococcygeus muscle) is a factor in the orgasmic dysfunction of millions of women. It used to be thought the problem was entirely of psychological origin, and in most cases it is. In some, however, it's simply a matter of poor muscle tone. Nearly 40 percent of American women register a lack of P.C. muscle control.

Control can easily be learned. In fact, knowledge of this muscle is common in other cultures and is frequently a part of marriage preparation. In one African tribe, for instance, no girl may marry until she is able to exert strong pressure with the vaginal muscles.[12]

If these exercises are faithfully applied, control can be developed in six to eight weeks. The muscle can be fully developed in about eight months, after which it can exert pressure on the penis like that of a clenched fist. It is then even possible for a woman to bring her husband to an orgasm while in the female above position by doing nothing but contracting this muscle—with no other movement. Thus, when you as a wife develop this muscle for your own benefit, it is also a definite factor in giving increased pleasure to your husband.[13]

How then can the P.C. muscle be developed? The best way to learn the feeling of the contraction is to remember that this is the muscle that holds back the flow of urine. However, there are other muscles besides the P.C. which also help control urine flow. In order to keep these other muscles out of the exercise, urine flow must be controlled with the knees widely separated. Once the flow has begun, make an effort to stop it. After a few trials, most women can recognize the sensation and can repeat the contractions anytime, anywhere. There is very little physical effort involved. Once the contraction is properly learned, it is no more difficult than blinking the eye.

You should begin every morning with five or ten contractions before arising. Work up to six contractions in a row, made at ten intervals a day. This totals sixty contractions. Each contraction should be held for about two seconds at this stage. Thus, sixty contractions involve a total of about two minutes a day.

Gradually the number of sessions should increase. Twenty contractions per session bring the total to 120 (four minutes a day). If this is done while urinating three times, as well as once before arising, once at some other time, and once after retiring, the total of 120 is reached. In six weeks you should work up to 300 contractions a day with fifty contractions at each of six intervals. Now, only hold the contractions for one second each instead of two. Thus, we are talking about a total of 300 seconds a day or a mere five minutes!

You should be able to note some sexual changes within three weeks. Full development can be achieved in six to eight weeks. If this exercise is kept up for nine months, gradually increasing to about 600 contractions a day (about 10 minutes), the vagina can be developed to give unusual pleasurable sensations to your husband during intercourse.

The value of this exercise is not only physical but psychological. It is helpful for a wife to fantasize about gripping her husband's penis while attempting the exercise. This cannot help but focus your mind on sexual thoughts and will likely increase your desire. Thus, this exercise becomes an excellent way of bringing your level of sexual desire up to your husband's. Furthermore, it can give a woman a sense of an "active" part in sexual intercourse. She no longer views herself as merely a passive recepticle. The P.C. muscle offers a concept of the vagina, not merely as a receiver of action, but as an actor.

It is very important that a woman struggling with frigidity have an active attitude toward achieving orgasm. She must eagerly reach out and strive for the orgasm. She can't just wait to see if it will happen. It is not selfish to reach out for this pleasure, and it is not wrong to think sexual thoughts about your husband during the day. Shulamith did (Song 5:10–16).

For a full explanation of the P.C. muscle and its place in sexual function, may I suggest you purchase *The Key to Feminine Response in Marriage* by Ronald M. Deutsch (New York: Random House, 1968).

STEP 10—*Develop tactile sensation without any intention of moving to orgasm.*

Some frigid women have absolutely no physical sensation in the vaginal area at all. They are not even conscious of sexually pleasurable feelings. This situation is mainly of psychological origin, but along with the psychological steps (Steps 1–8), these last four steps of a physical nature can be helpful. However, do not try to implement these physical procedures without first dealing as thoroughly as possible with the spiritual and psychological issues. Those are the foundation, and we are now discussing the superstructure.

As a woman learns to yield, genital sensations will gradually increase. It is helpful, however, for her to learn to feel sexually with external physical techniques also. This can be done in several ways. Have your husband give you a body massage. Make it long and loving. The purpose is simply

SOLOMON ON SEX

to help you become aware of sensual feelings. Love can be communicated by touch.

It is very important that both partners have a mutual agreement that the purpose of the session is not to bring the wife to an orgasm. If she feels she is supposed to climax as a result, the goal orientation will set in and may block her response. The goal at this stage is not to climax but simply to learn awareness of tactile feelings all over the body. Your wife might like you to draw fur or silk scarves across her body and breasts. Again the goal is simply a relaxed enjoyment of one another's presence, loving conversation, and learning to feel tactile sensations not necessarily of a sexual nature. Obviously, it will be necessary for the wife to bring her husband to a climax toward the end of the session either manually or through intercourse. But her orgasm is not to be considered part of the session unless for some reason she wants to.

STEP 11—*Practice structured genital sensation.*

Once tactile awareness is being built (perhaps after five or six sessions), Masters and Johnson suggest that structured genital stimulation begin. Once again, the goal is not orgasm, but learning to feel sexually. In Step 10, the genitals should be avoided. In this step they should be concentrated on. There must be no demand on the husband's part for his wife to achieve orgasm.

The husband sits leaning against pillows at the head of the bed with the woman seated between his legs, her back against his chest and her head resting on one of his shoulders. This position is conducive to a sense of security and trust as the husband's arms are felt around her. She separates her legs and extends them across her husband's legs. The husband now has full access to any part of her body. The wife should then place her hand lightly over her husband's so she can signal him to touch more lightly, heavily, or in a different place. Thus, she can communicate her wishes in a physical way without having to talk.

Clitoral stimulation should be along the side of the clitoral shaft rather than on the glans (head). Touching the glans (tip) of the clitoris too soon can reduce her sexual tension immediately or may actually cause pain. Start with light stroking motions on the breasts, belly and thighs, then to the genital area as the wife directs.

The effectiveness of this session is not in any way related to whether or not she achieves an orgasm, because once again, that is not the session's purpose. The purpose of this exercise is to give the woman a chance to focus on her own sexual feelings, to discover what her preferences are, and to communicate this information to her husband. When the wife knows that nothing is demanded of her, that she has complete freedom to express herself, and that she will soon have another chance for sexual activity, there is a buildup of sexual feeling that eventually will result in a climax. The response is impossible to will or to force.

STEP 12—*Intercourse in the female above position.* After three or four sessions of Step 10, shift to several sessions of actual intercourse in the woman astride position. Begin penetration very slowly; the wife must control it completely. She should hold herself still so she can savor the feelings of penetration without any demand to climax. Shortly after entry, she should begin to contract the P.C. muscle as this will help focus her sensations. As her sexual tension elevates and she wants more stimulation, she can move slowly back and forth on the penis for a brief time. Only after three or four sessions of this, or when sexually demanding feelings begin to develop in the vagina, should the man begin any pelvic thrusting. He should then thrust slowly and in a non-demanding manner, letting her determine the pace she prefers.

Obviously, this whole procedure will require the husband's total cooperation. He must demonstrate enormous amounts of self-giving love (as Christ loved the church) and sympathy, and live with his wife in a truly "understanding way" (1 Pet. 3:7). It will be necessary for the wife to satisfy her husband during each session, but her orgasm is not to be the objective until it just happens as the culmination of all the steps.

FOOTNOTES

1. Article in *Dallas Times Herald.*
2. Herbert Miles, *Sexual Happiness in Marriage* (Grand Rapids: Zondervan, 1967), p. 141.
3. Fred Belliveau and Lin Richter, *Understanding Human Sexual Inadequacy* (New York: Bantam Books, 1970), p. 122.
4. *Ibid.,* p. 111.
5. *Ibid.*
6. *Ibid.*, p. 122.
7. Marie Robinson, *The Power of Sexual Surrender* (New York: Signet Books, 1962), p. 132.
8. *Ibid.*, p. 133.
9. *Ibid.*, p. 137.
10. Arianna Stassinopoulos, *The Female Woman* (New York: Random House, 1973), pp. 18-19.
11. Robinson, pp. 152-153.
12. Ronald M. Deutsch, *The Key to Feminine Response in Marriage* (New York: Random House, 1968), p. 62.
13. *Ibid.*, p. 96.

APPENDIX II

The following is based on the King James Version of the Bible; obviously, you may substitute your favorite version as you read and study this appendix. An interpretive outline is interspersed throughout the text, and the speakers are designated in order to aid note-taking and understanding of the Song, and to supply a help for those desiring to teach the Song of Solomon.

I. The Wedding Day (1:1-2:7)

  A. Reflection #1: Shulamith in the Palace (1:2-8)
    This reflection opens the book with Shulamith in the palace, preparing for the wedding banquet that afternoon and the wedding night to follow.

    1:1 The Song of Songs, which is Solomon's

1:2 SHULAMITH:
Let him kiss me with the kisses of his mouth:
For thy love is better than wine.

1:3 Because of the savor of thy good ointments thy name is
as ointment poured forth,
Therefore do the virgins love thee.

1:4 Draw me, we will run after thee:
The king hath brought me into his chambers:

CHORUS:
We will be glad and rejoice in thee,
We will remember thy love more than wine:
The upright love thee.

1:5 I am black, but comely,
O ye daughters of Jerusalem,
As the tents of Kedar,
As the curtains of Solomon.

1:6 Look not upon me,
Because I am black,
Because the sun hath looked upon me:
My mother's children were angry with me;
They made me the keeper of the vineyards;
But mine own vineyard have I not kept.

1:7 Tell me, O thou whom my soul loveth,
Where thou feedest,
Where thou makest thy flock to rest at noon:
For why should I be as one that turneth aside by the
flocks of thy companions?

1:8 CHORUS:
If thou know not,
O thou fairest among women,
Go thy way forth by the footsteps of the flock,
And feed thy kids beside the shepherds' tents.

B. Reflection #2: At the Banquet Table (1:9–14)
Shulamith and Solomon recline at the wedding banquet and mutually praise one another's beauty.

1:9 SOLOMON:
I have compared thee, O my love,
To a company of horses in Pharoah's chariots.

1:10 Thy cheeks are comely with rows of jewels,
Thy neck with chains of gold.

1:11 We will make thee borders of gold with studs of silver.

SOLOMON ON SEX

1:12 While the King sitteth at his table,
　　My spikenard sendeth forth the smell thereof.
1:13 A bundle of myrrh is my well-beloved unto me;
　　He shall lie all night betwixt my breasts.
1:14 My beloved is unto me as a cluster of camphire in the
　　vineyards of En-gedi.

C. Reflection #3: In the Bridal Chamber (1:15-2:7)
　　Here the royal couple moves into the wedding chamber and spend their first night together. The details are specifically but tastefully told in the language of poetic symbolism.

1:15 SOLOMON:
　　Behold, thou art fair, my love;
　　Behold, thou art fair;
　　Thou hast doves' eyes.

1:16 SHULAMITH:
　　Behold, thou art fair, my beloved, yea, pleasant:
　　Also our bed is green.
1:17 The beams of our house are cedar,
　　And our rafters of fir.
2:1 I am the rose of Sharon,
　　And the lily of the valleys.

　　SOLOMON:
2:2 As the lily among thorns,
　　So is my love among the daughters.

2:3 SHULAMITH:
　　As the apple tree among the trees of the wood,
　　So is my beloved among the sons.
　　I sat down under his shadow with great delight,
　　And his fruit was sweet to my taste.
2:4 He brought me to the banqueting house,
　　And his banner over me was love.
2:5 Stay me with flagons,
　　Comfort me with apples:
　　For I am sick of love.
2:6 His left hand is under my head,
　　And his right hand doth embrace me.
2:7 I charge you, O ye daughters of Jerusalem,
　　By the roes, and by the hinds of the field,
　　That ye stir not up,
　　Nor awake my love, till he please.

II. The Courtship Days (2:8-3:5)

    A. Reflection #4: A Springtime Visit (2:8-14)

As Shulamith reflects on her wedding day, she remembers the spring-time visit Solomon paid to her country home in the Lebanon mountains. These three reflections occur as Shulamith awaits the wedding procession sent by Solomon to pick her up and bring her to the palace in Jerusalem. These reflections picture God's purposes in courtship. The first brings out the idea that God's primary purpose is that couples get to know one another in ways other than sexual.

2:8 SHULAMITH:
>The voice of my beloved!
>Behold, he cometh leaping upon the mountains,
>Skipping upon the hills.

2:9 My beloved is like a roe or a young hart:
>Behold, he standeth behind our wall,
>He looketh forth at the windows,
>Showing himself through the lattice.

2:10 SOLOMON:
>My beloved spake, and said unto me,
>Rise up, my love, my fair one,
>And come away.

2:11 For, lo, the winter is past,
>The rain is over and gone;

2:12 The flowers appear on the earth;
>The time of the singing of birds is come
>And the voice of the turtle is heard in our land;

2:13 The fig tree putteth forth her green figs,
>And the vines with the tender grape give a good smell.
>Arise, my love, my fair one,
>And come away.

2:14 O my dove,
>That art in the clefts of the rock,
>In the secret places of the stairs,
>Let me see thy countenance,
>Let me hear thy voice;
>For sweet is thy voice,
>And thy countenance is comely.

    B. Reflection #5: Catching the Little Foxes (2:15–17)

During their courtship days they take a walk in the vineyard and see foxes eating the roots of the vines. This suggests to Shulamith the necessity of working through little problems together before entering into marriage.

2:15 SHULAMITH:
    Take us the foxes,
    The little foxes, that spoil the vines:
    For our vines have tender grapes.
2:16 My beloved is mine,
    And I am his:
    He feedeth among the lilies.
2:17 Until the day break,
    And the shadows flee away,
    Turn, my beloved,
    And be thou like a roe or a young hart upon
        the mountains of Bether.

C. Reflection #6: A Dream of Separation (3:1-5)
    She remembers dreaming repeatedly of her fear that Solomon would be so engaged in the affairs of state that he would not have time for her.

3:1 SHULAMITH:
    By night on my bed I sought him whom my soul loveth:
    I sought him, but I found him not.
3:2 I will rise now,
    And go about the city in the streets,
    And in the broad ways I will seek him whom my soul loveth:
    I sought him, but I found him not.
3:3 The watchmen that go about the city found me:
    To whom I said,
    Saw ye him whom my soul loveth?
3:4 It was but a little that I passed from them,
    But I found him whom my soul loveth:
    I held him, and would not let him go,
    Until I had brought him into my mother's house,
    And into the chamber of her that conceived me.
3:5 I charge you, O ye daughters of Jerusalem,
    By the roes, and by the hinds of the field,
    That ye stir not up,
    Nor awake my love,
    Till he please.

III. From the Wedding Procession to Marital Union (3:6-5:1)

A. Reflection #7: The Wedding Procession (3:6-3:11)
    This reflection describes the elegant wedding procession Solomon

sent from Jerusalem to pick up his Shulamite bride in the Lebanon mountains.

3:6 CHORUS:
> Who is this that cometh out of the wilderness
>   like pillars of smoke,
> Perfumed with myrrh and frankincense,
> With all powders of the merchant?

3:7 Behold his bed,
> Which is Solomon's;
> Threescore valiant men are about it,
> Of the valiant of Israel.

3:8 They all hold swords,
> Being expert in war:
> Every man hath his sword upon his thigh because
>   of fear in the night.

3:9 King Solomon made himself a chariot of the wood of Lebanon.

3:10 He made the pillars thereof of silver,
> The bottom thereof of gold,
> The covering of it of purple,
> The midst thereof being paved with love,
> For the daughters of Jerusalem.

3:11 Go forth, O ye daughters of Zion,
> And behold King Solomon with the crown wherewith his
>   mother crowned him in the day of his espousals,
> And in the day of the gladness of his heart.

B. Reflection #8: The Royal Couple Alone on the Wedding Night (4:1-5:1)

Shulamith sings about the beauty of their first night together and we get a sacred look into the bedroom, viewing God's attitudes toward sex in marriage.

4:1 SOLOMON:
> Behold, thou art fair, my love;
> Behold, thou art fair;
> Thou hast doves' eyes within thy locks:
> Thy hair is as a flock of goats,
> That appear from mount Gilead.

4:2 Thy teeth are like a flock of sheep that are even shorn,
> Which came up from the washing;
> Whereof every one bear twins,
> And none is barren among them.

4:3 Thy lips are like a thread of scarlet,
> And thy speech is comely:

SOLOMON ON SEX

Thy temples are like a piece of a pomegranate within thy locks.

4:4 Thy neck is like the tower of David builded for an armory,
Whereon there hang a thousand bucklers,
All shields of mighty men.

4:5 Thy two breasts are like two young roes that are twins,
Which feed among the lilies.

4:6 Until the day break,
And the shadows flee away,
I will get me to the mountain of myrrh,
And to the hill of frankincense.

4:7 Thou art all fair, my love;
There is no spot in thee.

4:8 Come with me from Lebanon, my spouse,
With me from Lebanon:
Look from the top of Amana,
From the top of Shenir and Hermon,
From the lions' dens,
From the mountains of the leopards.

4:9 Thou hast ravished my heart, my sister, my spouse;
Thou hast ravished my heart with one of thine eyes,
With one chain of thy neck.

4:10 How fair is thy love, my sister, my spouse!
How much better is thy love than wine!
And the smell of thine ointments than all spices!

4:11 Thy lips, O my spouse,
Drop as the honeycomb:
Honey and milk are under thy tongue;
And the smell of thy garments is like the smell of Lebanon.

4:12 A garden inclosed is my sister, my spouse;
A spring shut up,
A fountain sealed.

4:13 Thy plants are an orchard of pomegranates,
With pleasant fruits;
Camphire, with spikenard,

4:14 Spikenard and saffron;
Calamus and cinnamon,
With all trees of frankincense;
Myrrh and aloes,
With all the chief spices:

4:15 A fountain of gardens,
A well of living waters,
And streams from Lebanon.

4:16 SHULAMITH:
Awake, O north wind;
And come, thou south;
Blow upon my garden,
That the spices thereof may flow out.
Let my beloved come into his garden,
And eat his pleasant fruits.

5:1 SOLOMON:
I am come into my garden, my sister, my spouse:
I have gathered my myrrh with my spice;
I have eaten my honeycomb with my honey;
I have drunk my wine with my milk.

THE LORD:
Eat, O friends;
Drink, yea, drink abundantly, O beloved.

IV. Sexual Adjustments in Marriage: "The Dream of Love's Refusal"
to the "Dance of the Mahanaim" (5:2-8:4)

A. Reflection #9: Here we enter Shulamith's troubled and dream-filled
sleep. She dreams repeatedly of refusing Solomon's sexual advances
late at night, and seems troubled about her responses (5:2-5:8).

5:2 SHULAMITH:
I sleep, but my heart waketh:
It is the voice of my beloved that knocketh, saying

SOLOMON:
Open to me, my sister, my love, my dove, my undefiled:
For my head is filled with dew,
And my locks with the drops of the night.

5:3 SHULAMITH:
I have put off my coat;
How shall I put it on?
I have washed my feet;
How shall I defile them?

5:4 My beloved put in his hand by the hole of the door,
And my bowels were moved for him.

5:5 I rose up to open to my beloved;
And my hands dropped with myrrh,
And my fingers with sweet smelling myrrh,
Upon the handles of the lock.

SOLOMON ON SEX

5:6 I opened to my beloved;
       By my beloved had withdrawn himself, and was gone:
       My soul failed when he spake:
       I sought him, but I could not find him;
       I called him, but he gave me no answer.

5:7 The watchmen that went about the city found me,
       They smote me, they wounded me;
       The keepers of the walls took away my veil from me.

5:8 I charge you, O daughters of Jerusalem, ·
       If ye find my beloved,
       That ye tell him,
       That I am sick of love.

B. Reflection #10: A Change of Attitude (5:9-6:3)

    As she awakens the next day, Shulamith changes her attitude about sex and about her husband's availability. This is the beginning of their deepened relationship.

5:9 CHORUS:
       What is thy beloved more than another beloved,
       O thou fairest among women?
       What is thy beloved more than another beloved,
       That thou dost so charge us?

5:10 SHULAMITH:
       My beloved is white and ruddy,
       The chiefest among ten thousand.

5:11 His head is as the most fine gold;
       His locks are bushy,
       And black as a raven:

5:12 His eyes are as the eyes of doves by the rivers
         of waters,
       Washed with milk,
       And fitly set:

5:13 His cheeks are as a bed of spices,
       As sweet flowers:
       His lips like lilies,
       Dropping sweet smelling myrrh:

5:14 His hands are as gold rings set with the beryl:
       His belly is as bright ivory overlaid with sapphires;

5:15 His legs are as pillars of marble,
       Set upon sockets of fine gold:
       His countenance is as Lebanon,
       Excellent as the cedars:

5:16 His mouth is most sweet:
Yea, he is altogether lovely.
This is my beloved,
And this is my friend, O daughters of Jerusalem.

6:1 CHORUS:
Whither is thy beloved gone, O thou fairest among women?
Whither is thy beloved turned aside?
That we may seek him with thee.

6:2 SHULAMITH:
My beloved is gone down into his garden,
To the bed of spices,
To feed in the gardens,
And to gather lilies.

6:3 I am my beloved's,
And my beloved is mine:
He feedeth among the lilies.

C. Reflection #11: The Return of Solomon (6:4–10)
Solomon returns from business of state and reflects his praise and unconditional acceptance of Shulamith in spite of the problems they have been having in sexual adjustment.

6:4 SOLOMON:
Thou art beautiful, O my love, as Tirzah,
Comely as Jerusalem,
Terrible as an army with banners.

6:5 Turn away thine eyes from me,
For they have overcome me:
Thy hair is as a flock of goats that appear from Gilead:

6:6 Thy teeth are as a flock of sheep which go up
from the washing,
Whereof every one beareth twins,
And there is not one barren among them.

6:7 As a piece of pomegranate are thy temples
within thy locks.

6:8 There are threescore queens,
And fourscore concubines
And virgins without number.

6:9 My dove, my undefiled is but one;
She is the only one of her mother,
She is the choice one of her that bare her.
The daughters saw her, and blessed her;

Yea, the queens and the concubines,
And they praised her.
6:10 Who is she that looketh forth as the morning,
Fair as the moon,
Clear as the sun,
And terrible as an army with banners?

D. Reflection #12: Shulamith in the Garden (6:11-13a)
   The second problem on Shulamith's heart was her longing for her country home. She was a country girl in the palace of the king. She visits the palace gardens, and suddenly her heart longs for the country she loves.

6:11 SHULAMITH:
I went down into the garden of nuts
To see the fruits of the valley,
And to see whether the vine flourished,
And the pomegranates budded.
6:12 Or ever I was aware,
My soul made me like the chariots of Amminadib.

6:7:13a CHORUS:
Return, return, O Shulamite;
Return, return, that we may look upon thee.

E. Reflection#13: The Dance of the Mahanaim (6:12b–8:4)
   Here she reflects on another love experience that came at the conclusions of the tensions described in the preceding three reflections. In this reflection she recalls dancing before Solomon as part of their loveplay. Solomon responds by extolling her beauty.

6:13b SHULAMITH (TO THE CHORUS):
What will ye see in the Shulamite?
As it were the company of two armies.

7:1 SOLOMON:
How beautiful are thy feet with shoes,
   O prince's daughter!
The joints of thy thighs are like jewels,
The work of the hands of a cunning workman.
7:2 Thy navel is like a round goblet,
Which wanteth not liquor:
Thy belly is like a heap of wheat set about with lilies.
7:3 Thy two breasts are like two young roes that are twins.
7:4 Thy neck is as a tower of ivory;
Thine eyes like the fishpools in Heshbon,

By the gate of Bath-rabbim:
Thy nose is as the tower of Lebanon which looketh
toward Damascus.

7:5 Thine head upon thee is like Carmel,
And the hair of thine head like purple;
The king is held in the galleries.

7:6 How fair and how pleasant art thou,
O love, for delights!

7:7 This thy stature is like to a palm tree,
And thy breasts to clusters of grapes.

7:8 I said, I will go up to the palm tree,
I will take hold of the boughs thereof:
Now also thy breasts shall be as clusters of the vine,
And the smell of thy nose like apples;

7:9a And the roof of thy mouth like the best wine
for my beloved,

7:9b SHULAMITH:
That goeth down sweetly,
Causing the lips of those that are asleep to speak.

7:10 I am my beloved's,
And his desire is toward me.

7:11 Come, my beloved,
Let us go forth into the field;
Let us lodge in the villages.

7:12 Let us get up early to the vineyards;
Let us see if the vine flourish,
Whether the tender grape appear,
And the pomegranates bud forth:
There will I give thee my loves.

7:13 The mandrakes give a smell,
And at our gates are all manner of pleasant fruits,
New and old,
Which I have laid up for thee, O my beloved.

8:1 O that thou wert as my brother,
That sucked the breasts of my mother!
When I should find thee without,
I would kiss thee;
Yea, I should not be despised.

8:2 I would lead thee,
And bring thee into my mother's house,
Who would instruct me:
I would cause thee to drink of spiced wine
of the juice of my pomegranate.

SOLOMON ON SEX

8:3 His left hand should be under my head,
And his right hand should embrace me.
8:4 I charge you, O daughters of Jerusalem,
That ye stir not up,
Nor awake my love,
Until he please.

V. A Vacation in the Country (8:5–14)

A. Reflection #14: The Journey to the Mountains (8:5-14)
   Part of the solution to the tensions they had been feeling was a need to get away together. Shulamith suggests a vacation in the mountains, and this reflection recalls their conversation as they journey. It is here that the kind of love they have experienced is first explained to the reader.

8:5a CHORUS:
Who is this that cometh up from the wilderness,
Leaning upon her beloved?

8:5b SOLOMON:
I raised thee up under the apple tree:
There thy mother brought thee forth;
There she brought thee forth that bare thee.

8:6 SHULAMITH:
Set me as a seal upon thine heart,
As a seal upon thine arm:
For love is strong as death;
Jealousy is cruel as the grave:
The coals thereof are coals of fire,
Which hath a most vehement flame.
8:7 Many waters cannot quench love,
Neither can the floods drown it:
If a man would give all the substance of his house
for love,
It would utterly be condemned.

In their conversation it appears that true love has two characteristics: it is intense and it is unconditional. The question that naturally comes to the mind of the readers is, "How can such love be obtained?"

In the concluding conversation, the poet answers this question by relating some events from Shulamith's home life. In a "flashback" concerning how to keep her chaste and pure.

8:8 SHULAMITH'S BROTHERS (AMONG THEMSELVES):
We have a little sister,
And she hath no breasts:
What shall we do for our sister in the day when
she shall be spoken for?
8:9 If she be a wall,
We will build upon her a palace of silver:
And if she be a door,
We will inclose her with boards of cedar.

8:10 SHULAMITH:
I am a wall,
And my breasts like towers:
Then was I in his eyes as one that found favor.
8:11 Solomon had a vineyard at Baal-hamon;
He let out the vineyard unto keepers;
Every one for the fruit thereof was to bring a thousand
pieces of silver.
8:12 My vineyard,
Which is mine,
Is before me:
Thou, O Solomon, must have a thousand,
And those that keep the fruit thereof two hundred.

8:13 SOLOMON:
Thou that dwellest in the gardens,
The companions hearken to thy voice:
Cause me to hear it.

8:14 SHULAMITH:
Make haste, my beloved,
And be thou like to a roe or to a young hart upon
the mountains of spices.

SOLOMON ON SEX

THE SONG OF SOLOMON

THE BEGINNING OF LOVE			THE DEVELOPMENT OF ONENESS		
THE WEDDING DAY	REFLECTIONS ON A COURTSHIP	THE WEDDING DAY	A DREAM OF LOVE REFUSED		A VACATION IN THE COUNTRY
			A PROBLEM	THE SOLUTION	
	(a parenthesis)	(continued)			
1. Shulamith in the Palace (1:1–8) 2. At the Banquet Table (1:9–14) 3. In the Bridal Chamber (1:15–2:7)	4. A Springtime Visit (2:8–11) 5. The Little Foxes (2:15–17) 6. A Dream—On Counting the Cost (3:1–5)	7. The Wedding Procession (3:6–11) 8. The Wedding Night (4:1–5:1)	9. A Dream of Love Refused (5:2–8)	10. A Change of Attitude (5:9–6:3) 11. The Return of Solomon (6:4–10) 12. Shulamith in the Garden (6:11–13a) 13. The Dance of the Mahanaim (6:13b–8:4)	14. A Vacation in the Country (8:5–14)
1:1 2:7	2:8 3:5	3:6 5:1	5:2 5:8	5:9 8:4	8:5 8:14
THE GLORIOUS IDEAL			THE PRACTICAL REALITY		
LOVE'S FIRST ENTRANCING DAYS			LOVE'S DEEP ABIDING JOYS		
PALACE	LEBANON		PALACE		LEBANON